THE GOLDEN BOOK OF
CRAFTS AND HOBBIES

by W. BEN HUNT

 GOLDEN PRESS · NEW YORK

Western Publishing Company, Inc.
Racine, Wisconsin

Library of Congress Catalog Card Number: 57-14089

Sixteenth Printing, 1972

CONTENTS

The back part of Ben Hunt's cabin is his workshop and storage shed.

About This Book

This book contains a number of projects suitable for boys and girls to do either by themselves or under the direction of scout leaders, camp instructors, or school teachers. All of the projects have been carefully designed and personally made by the author. Most of the projects have been tested in camps and by boy and girl scout troops.

All of the drawings are clear and complete, and most of the articles can be made with a few simple tools and materials that are easily obtained. In fact, many can be completed with little more than a good pocketknife.

The plans in this book and the suggestions for materials to be used do not have to be followed exactly. In some cases you may have to use substitutes.

It is a lot of fun to work out handicraft projects with a chum or a group of friends, because then you can use each other's tools and help one another with the difficult parts.

Your workshop can be your basement, a spare room, a kitchen table, or even outdoors. A basement or barn workshop is usually the best because it can be fitted up with very little expense and is out of the way. Your most expensive equipment will probably be your workbench. It should be strong enough to hold a three- or four-inch vise.

To make a work shack of cedar posts, remove the bark from the posts with a drawknife.

Whittling

Whittling is an art that has been practiced for many centuries. Many fine carvings have been made with just a pocketknife.

There are four prerequisites for good whittling: 1. A good two- or three-bladed pocketknife with a handle about 3½ inches long. It should have one large, strong blade and one or two smaller blades. 2. An oil stone or whetstone for sharpening the knife. 3. The right kind of wood for whittling. White pine, basswood, cottonwood, cedar, poplar, and willow are the best, for they all have straight grains. 4. Some idea in your head as to what you want to make.

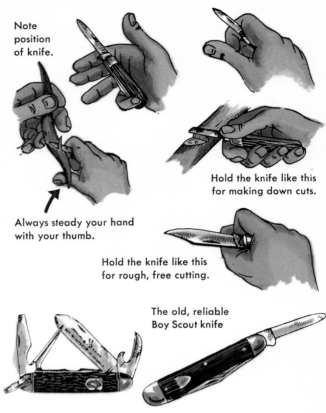

This is the correct way to hold a pocketknife for ordinary whittling. You get better leverage by holding knife part way up on the blade.

Note position of knife.

Always steady your hand with your thumb.

Hold the knife like this for making down cuts.

Hold the knife like this for rough, free cutting.

The old, reliable Boy Scout knife

Don't lay your knife down when you are finished with it. Always close it up and put it in your pocket.

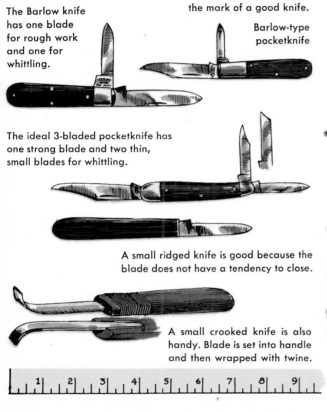

The Barlow knife has one blade for rough work and one for whittling.

A strong spring is usually the mark of a good knife.

Barlow-type pocketknife

The ideal 3-bladed pocketknife has one strong blade and two thin, small blades for whittling.

A small ridged knife is good because the blade does not have a tendency to close.

A small crooked knife is also handy. Blade is set into handle and then wrapped with twine.

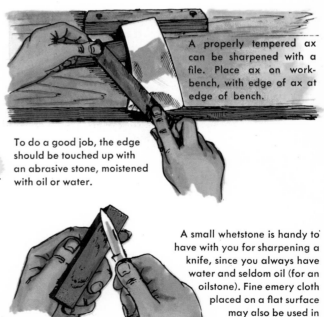

A properly tempered ax can be sharpened with a file. Place ax on workbench, with edge of ax at edge of bench.

To do a good job, the edge should be touched up with an abrasive stone, moistened with oil or water.

A small whetstone is handy to have with you for sharpening a knife, since you always have water and seldom oil (for an oilstone). Fine emery cloth placed on a flat surface may also be used in the same manner.

Here are a few rules to keep in mind when whittling: 1. Always keep your knife blade sharp and clean. 2. When you finish whittling, always close up your knife and put it in your pocket. 3. Never try to whittle hardwood or woods that contain resins. 4. Don't use your knife to open cans, scrape metal, or pry things open or apart, or you will ruin the blade.

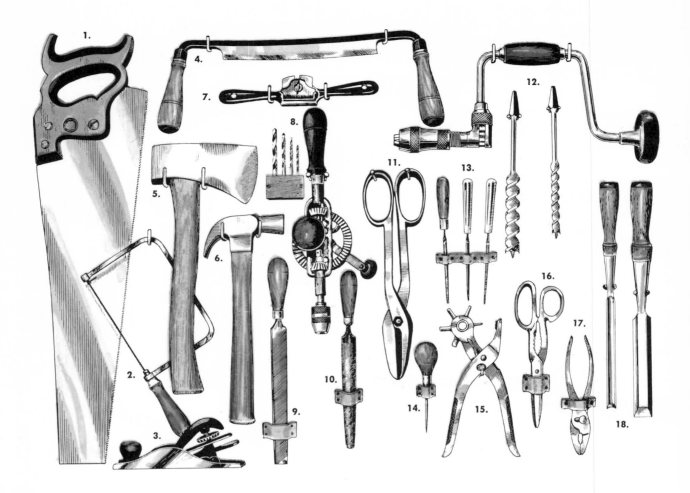

Tools and Materials

In addition to the knives shown on page 5, some of the basic tools that you will need for the projects in this book are pictured above:

1. saw	10. half-round file
2. coping saw	11. tin snips
3. plane	12. brace and bits
4. drawknife	13. screwdrivers
5. hand ax	14. awl
6. hammer	15. leather punch
7. spokeshave	16. shears
8. hand drill	17. pliers
9. file	18. chisel

The aluminum jewelry will require a few needle files and some stamping tools, which you can make yourself from large nails or spikes.

Most of these tools are part of every household. Those that you are missing your friends will probably have.

Materials are usually a little more difficult to obtain than tools. Sometimes a project will have to be delayed until you find just the right material.

The Indians and early settlers made their buckskin from tanned deerskin. After working brains and liver into the fresh hide, they smoke-tanned it over a small fire. The pitch from the smoke entered the fibers of the hide and prevented it from becoming hard and stiff, even after being wet. Today, commercial tanned buckskin, called chrome-tanned, is tanned with chemicals. It is also soft and pliable, but usually dries stiff and hard after it has been wet.

Split cowhide may be purchased from leather tanneries or leather supply houses. Be sure to specify the color you want; yellow, cream, or gray are best for most handicraft projects.

Because rawhide is difficult to obtain commercially, you might want to make your own. It is not hard to do, nor is it as smelly as you would imagine, providing you dispose of the scraps of flesh and hair, and work it outdoors.

First secure a fresh green cowhide from your butcher. Trim off all surplus flesh and fat with a sharp knife, being careful not to cut through the skin. Then lay the hide with the hair side up on a clean surface and sprinkle the top with a one-inch layer of dry wood ash. (Make wood ashes by simply burning a log of wood until it is entirely consumed by the fire.) Work the ash well into the hair and then sprinkle with soft water. Work the paste that is formed well into the hair. Then fold the hide into a bundle with the hair side in, and tie securely with a rope. Dig a hole in moist earth and cover with soil to keep the outside portions of the bundled hide from drying out.

After three or four days, unroll the hide, and the hair should come out easily. Rinse the hide in soft water. Lay the hide over a log and scrape off the hair as shown below. After the hide has been scraped of all hair, rinse it again in clear soft water and wring out as much water as possible. Stretch the hide as tight as possible on a wooden frame, as shown below. Set the frame in a shady place where air can circulate freely around the hide until it becomes bone dry. If you want your rawhide to be smooth, you can go over the surface with a piece of fine sandpaper or a flat pumice stone.

After it has dried, the rawhide can be cut into strips for lacing, or large flat pieces for tomtoms or drum heads. Rawhide must be kept dry because it has a tendency to mildew. When you are ready to work with a piece of hide, cut off the necessary amount and soak it until it is soft and pliable. It can then be stretched out, and when it dries, it will become as tight and hard as a piece of sheet steel. You can keep moisture out of finished work by giving it a coat of spar varnish or shellac.

Most of the other materials you will need can be found right at home.

This is the simplest frame for drying buckskin that you can make.

Drive blade halfway into wooden handle. Sharpen back of knife blade as you would sharpen a skate blade. This gives you two good sharp scraping edges.

Scraping hair off hide

7

Collecting and Mounting Insects

Insect collecting is an interesting hobby. Specimens can be found in every lot, field, garden, lake, and pond near your home.

After killing the insects, remove them from the killing jar and place them carefully in specimen envelopes. Label the envelopes for later identification. Until you have time to add them to your collection, store these envelopes in a small box so that the insects will not be crushed.

When you are ready to mount your specimens, put them in a relaxing jar, as shown, to make their wings soft and pliable enough to spread out. This will take from one to three days.

After they are completely relaxed, place the specimens on the spreading board and fasten them down to dry in the correct position. Wait at least a day or two to be sure your specimens are completely dry. Otherwise, they will fold back up into their original positions.

Get yourself a good reference book, such as the *Golden Nature Guide of Insects* by Zim, which will help you identify your specimens.

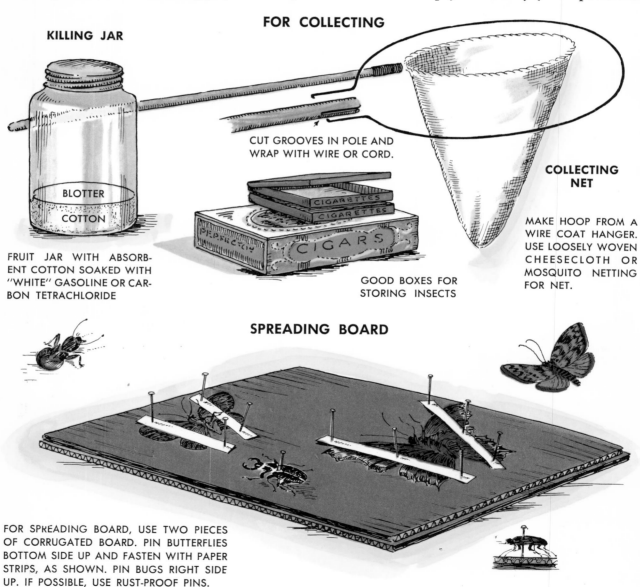

FOR COLLECTING

KILLING JAR

CUT GROOVES IN POLE AND WRAP WITH WIRE OR CORD.

COLLECTING NET

FRUIT JAR WITH ABSORBENT COTTON SOAKED WITH "WHITE" GASOLINE OR CARBON TETRACHLORIDE

GOOD BOXES FOR STORING INSECTS

MAKE HOOP FROM A WIRE COAT HANGER. USE LOOSELY WOVEN CHEESECLOTH OR MOSQUITO NETTING FOR NET.

BLOTTER

COTTON

SPREADING BOARD

FOR SPREADING BOARD, USE TWO PIECES OF CORRUGATED BOARD. PIN BUTTERFLIES BOTTOM SIDE UP AND FASTEN WITH PAPER STRIPS, AS SHOWN. PIN BUGS RIGHT SIDE UP. IF POSSIBLE, USE RUST-PROOF PINS.

DISPLAY BOXES

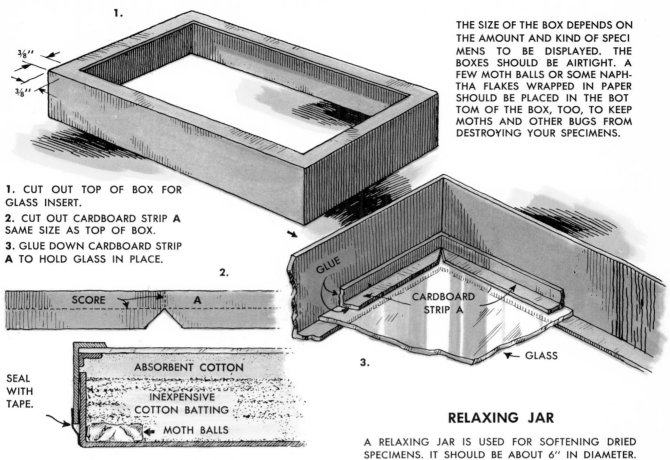

1.

3/8″
3/8″

THE SIZE OF THE BOX DEPENDS ON THE AMOUNT AND KIND OF SPECIMENS TO BE DISPLAYED. THE BOXES SHOULD BE AIRTIGHT. A FEW MOTH BALLS OR SOME NAPHTHA FLAKES WRAPPED IN PAPER SHOULD BE PLACED IN THE BOTTOM OF THE BOX, TOO, TO KEEP MOTHS AND OTHER BUGS FROM DESTROYING YOUR SPECIMENS.

1. CUT OUT TOP OF BOX FOR GLASS INSERT.

2. CUT OUT CARDBOARD STRIP **A** SAME SIZE AS TOP OF BOX.

3. GLUE DOWN CARDBOARD STRIP **A** TO HOLD GLASS IN PLACE.

2.

SCORE   A

GLUE

CARDBOARD STRIP A

3.

GLASS

SEAL WITH TAPE.

ABSORBENT COTTON

INEXPENSIVE COTTON BATTING

MOTH BALLS

RELAXING JAR

A RELAXING JAR IS USED FOR SOFTENING DRIED SPECIMENS. IT SHOULD BE ABOUT 6″ IN DIAMETER. FILL WITH 1″ TO 2″ OF SAND MOISTENED WITH WATER AND A FEW DROPS OF CARBOLIC ACID TO PREVENT MOLD.

SPECIMEN ENVELOPE

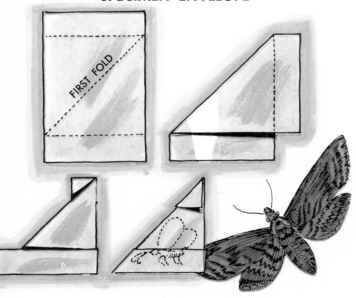

FIRST FOLD

WAXED PAPER

MAKE ENVELOPES FOR CARRYING HOME FIELD SPECIMENS. FIRST FOLD SHEET OF PAPER INTO ENVELOPE. THEN OPEN UP, PLACE SPECIMEN INSIDE, AND CLOSE.

Displaying Minerals and Shells

A collection of rocks or shells is more valuable if it is well labeled and properly displayed.

Visit your local museum or consult a guidebook for ideas on how to arrange your collection. Label each specimen with its scientific and common name. Also keep a detailed record of each specimen, listing both the scientific and common names, scientific classification, and where it was found.

Your specimens of rocks and minerals should be no larger than a walnut. Smaller shells will fit nicely in the compartments of the display case shown here. For larger shells you will have to make individual cases.

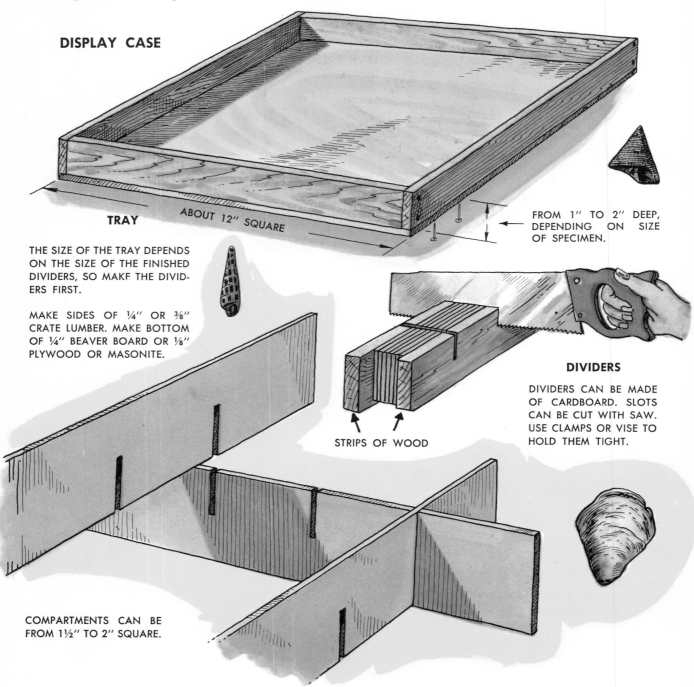

DISPLAY CASE

TRAY

ABOUT 12" SQUARE

FROM 1" TO 2" DEEP, DEPENDING ON SIZE OF SPECIMEN.

THE SIZE OF THE TRAY DEPENDS ON THE SIZE OF THE FINISHED DIVIDERS, SO MAKE THE DIVIDERS FIRST.

MAKE SIDES OF ¼" OR ⅜" CRATE LUMBER. MAKE BOTTOM OF ¼" BEAVER BOARD OR ⅛" PLYWOOD OR MASONITE.

STRIPS OF WOOD

DIVIDERS

DIVIDERS CAN BE MADE OF CARDBOARD. SLOTS CAN BE CUT WITH SAW. USE CLAMPS OR VISE TO HOLD THEM TIGHT.

COMPARTMENTS CAN BE FROM 1½" TO 2" SQUARE.

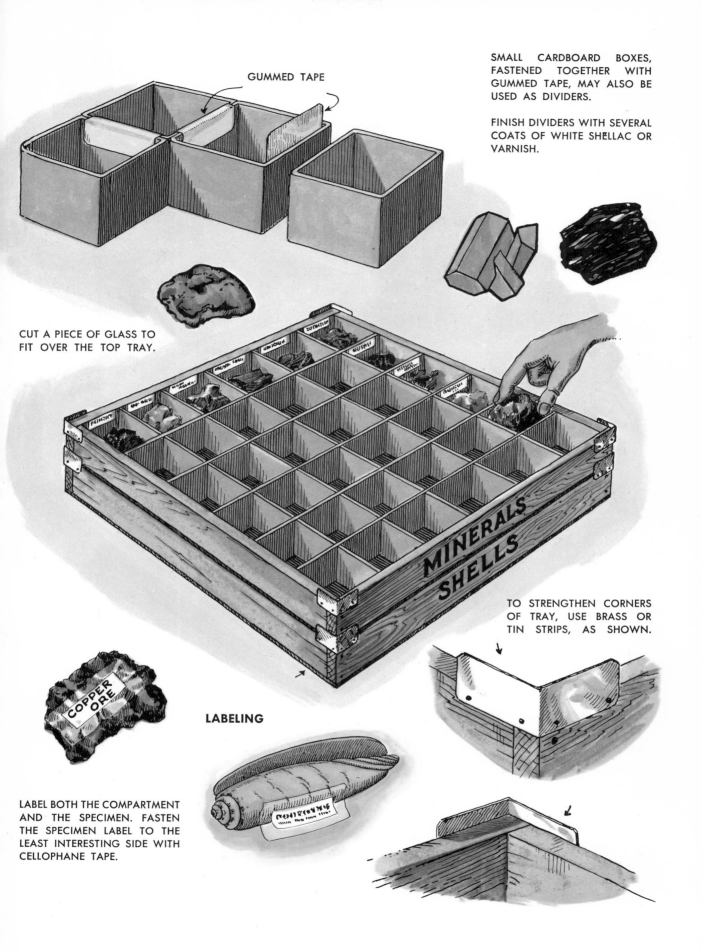

GUMMED TAPE

SMALL CARDBOARD BOXES, FASTENED TOGETHER WITH GUMMED TAPE, MAY ALSO BE USED AS DIVIDERS.

FINISH DIVIDERS WITH SEVERAL COATS OF WHITE SHELLAC OR VARNISH.

CUT A PIECE OF GLASS TO FIT OVER THE TOP TRAY.

MINERALS
SHELLS

COPPER ORE

TO STRENGTHEN CORNERS OF TRAY, USE BRASS OR TIN STRIPS, AS SHOWN.

LABELING

LABEL BOTH THE COMPARTMENT AND THE SPECIMEN. FASTEN THE SPECIMEN LABEL TO THE LEAST INTERESTING SIDE WITH CELLOPHANE TAPE.

SOOT AND INK PRINTING

1. APPLY A GOOD COAT OF SOOT TO A SHEET OF GREASED PAPER, OR

DAMPEN ALL DRY PRESSED LEAVES BEFORE INKING.

—APPLY PRINTING INK TO SHEET OF PAPER WITH SOFT LEATHER DAUBER OR RUBBER ROLLER.

2. PLACE LEAF FACE UP ON INKED SHEET OF PAPER (SINCE BACK OF LEAF USUALLY MAKES BEST PRINT). LAY A SHEET OF PAPER OVER IT AND RUB WITH FINGERTIPS TO INK LEAF.

3. THEN CLAMP TWO CLEAN SHEETS OF PAPER TOGETHER. PLACE INKED LEAF BETWEEN THEM, INKED SIDE DOWN, AND RUB. HOLD DOWN OVER STEM TO AVOID SHIFTING.

FOR SOOT OR INK PRINTING, YOU WILL NEED: A CANDLE OR A TUBE OF BLACK PRINTING INK; SHEETS OF HEAVY PAPER, ABOUT 8½" BY 11"; AND A SMALL INK ROLLER.

SOOT PRINT IN LOOSELEAF BINDER

Leaf Prints

Trees are interesting to observe all year round. In the winter, when all of the foliage is gone, you can study the characteristic shape, the arrangement of branches, the bark, and the winter buds. In the spring the opening of the leaf and flower buds is an amazing sight. Summer and fall, however, are the best times for collecting leaves.

Several ways to make a permanent leaf collection are shown on these two pages.

TO PRESERVE LEAVES, MOUNT THEM ON CARDBOARD WITH ⅛" STRIPS OF GUMMED TAPE. COVER CARDBOARD COMPLETELY WITH CLEAR CELLOPHANE.

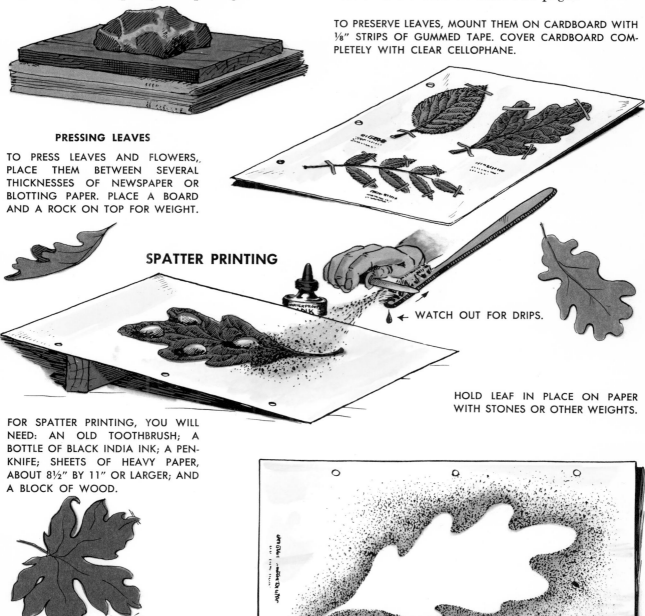

PRESSING LEAVES

TO PRESS LEAVES AND FLOWERS, PLACE THEM BETWEEN SEVERAL THICKNESSES OF NEWSPAPER OR BLOTTING PAPER. PLACE A BOARD AND A ROCK ON TOP FOR WEIGHT.

SPATTER PRINTING

← WATCH OUT FOR DRIPS.

HOLD LEAF IN PLACE ON PAPER WITH STONES OR OTHER WEIGHTS.

FOR SPATTER PRINTING, YOU WILL NEED: AN OLD TOOTHBRUSH; A BOTTLE OF BLACK INDIA INK; A PEN-KNIFE; SHEETS OF HEAVY PAPER, ABOUT 8½" BY 11" OR LARGER; AND A BLOCK OF WOOD.

FINISHED SPATTER PRINT

Plaster Casts

Plaster casts can be made of animal, bird or reptile tracks, leaves, and plants.

The only materials you will need are: modeling clay, cardboard, and a few pounds of plaster of Paris. Keep the plaster in a moisture-proof can or it will harden.

CASTS OF TRACKS

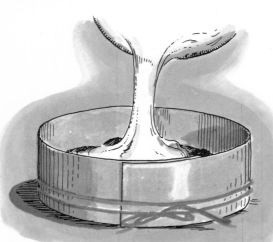

1. PREPARE TRACK BY PLACING A WALL OF CARDBOARD OR TIN AROUND IT.

2. MIX ONLY AS MUCH PLASTER OF PARIS AS YOU THINK YOU WILL NEED. SIFT IT INTO A BOWL OR CAN UNTIL SATURATION POINT IS REACHED. THEN SPRINKLE A LITTLE DRY PLASTER OVER THE TOP.

3. WHEN SMALL CRACKS APPEAR, STIR WELL AND POUR OVER TRACK TO ABOUT ½" OR ¾" DEPTH ABOVE GROUND LEVEL.

4. WHEN SET, LIFT OUT MOLD AND WASH OFF DIRT WITH WATER. THIS GIVES YOU A NEGATIVE IMPRESSION. TAKE THE MOLD BACK TO CAMP TO MAKE A POSITIVE CAST.

FINISHED CAST

5. TO MAKE POSITIVE CAST, SOAK NEGATIVE, BRUSHING IT WITH SOAPY WATER. TIE CARDBOARD WALL AROUND CAST AND POUR PLASTER. LET IT SET FOR 15 OR 20 MINUTES.

6. TRIM EDGES OF FINISHED CAST WITH A KNIFE.

CASTS OF LEAVES, PLANTS, AND GRASSES

FOR FLAT GREEN LEAVES OR PRESSED LEAVES

1. MOISTEN LEAF AND LAY IT ON FLAT SURFACE. FIRST BE SURE THAT EDGES ARE FLAT, OR PLASTER WILL RUN UNDER LEAF. THEN FOLLOW STEP 2 IN COLUMN BELOW.

FOR CURLED LEAVES

1. CURLED LEAVES THAT DO NOT LIE FLAT MAY BE PRESSED FIRST, OR LAID ON WET CLAY OR MUD. CLAY OR MUD IS THEN PLASTERED AROUND THE CURLED EDGES TO PREVENT PLASTER FROM RUNNING UNDER LEAF.

FOR TWIGS OF EVERGREENS, HARD LEAVES, OR GRASSES

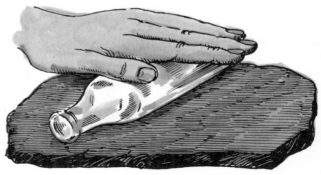

1. WITH A SMOOTH ROLLER, FLATTEN OUT SOME PLASTICINE OR MODELING CLAY.

2. LAY TWIG ON CLAY, FACE DOWN. PLACE A PIECE OF CARDBOARD OVER TWIG AND PRESS DOWN ON IT EVENLY AND FIRMLY.

3. LIFT CARDBOARD AND REMOVE TWIG SLOWLY. NOW YOU HAVE A NEGATIVE MOLD.

4. PLACE WALL OF CARDBOARD OR TIN AROUND CLAY. POUR PLASTER OF PARIS INTO MOLD. NOW YOU HAVE A POSITIVE MOLD OF TWIG.

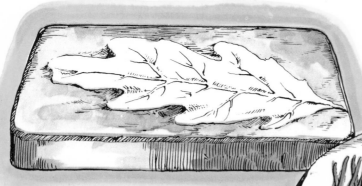

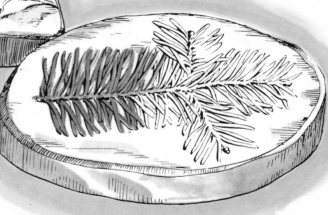

FINISHED CASTS

2. WHEN ALL EDGES ARE SEALED, PLACE WALL OF CARDBOARD OR TIN AROUND LEAF. POUR PLASTER TO CAST NEGATIVE MOLD.

3. TO MAKE POSITIVE, PLACE WALL AROUND NEGATIVE AND POUR PLASTER INTO MOLD.

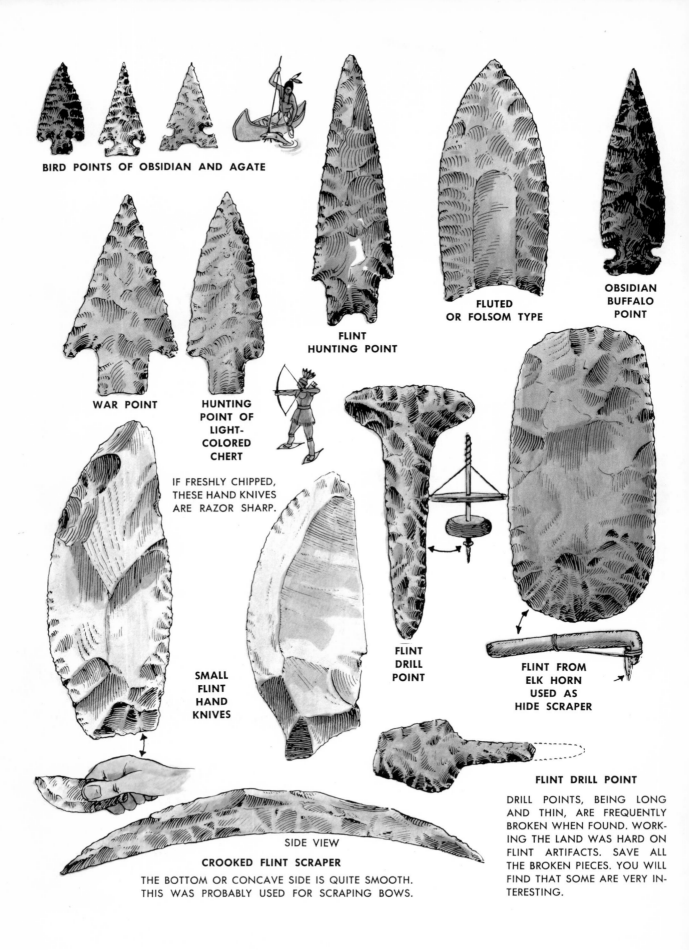

BIRD POINTS OF OBSIDIAN AND AGATE

FLINT
HUNTING POINT

FLUTED
OR FOLSOM TYPE

OBSIDIAN
BUFFALO
POINT

WAR POINT

HUNTING
POINT OF
LIGHT-
COLORED
CHERT

IF FRESHLY CHIPPED,
THESE HAND KNIVES
ARE RAZOR SHARP.

SMALL
FLINT
HAND
KNIVES

FLINT
DRILL
POINT

FLINT FROM
ELK HORN
USED AS
HIDE SCRAPER

SIDE VIEW

CROOKED FLINT SCRAPER

THE BOTTOM OR CONCAVE SIDE IS QUITE SMOOTH.
THIS WAS PROBABLY USED FOR SCRAPING BOWS.

FLINT DRILL POINT

DRILL POINTS, BEING LONG
AND THIN, ARE FREQUENTLY
BROKEN WHEN FOUND. WORK-
ING THE LAND WAS HARD ON
FLINT ARTIFACTS. SAVE ALL
THE BROKEN PIECES. YOU WILL
FIND THAT SOME ARE VERY IN-
TERESTING.

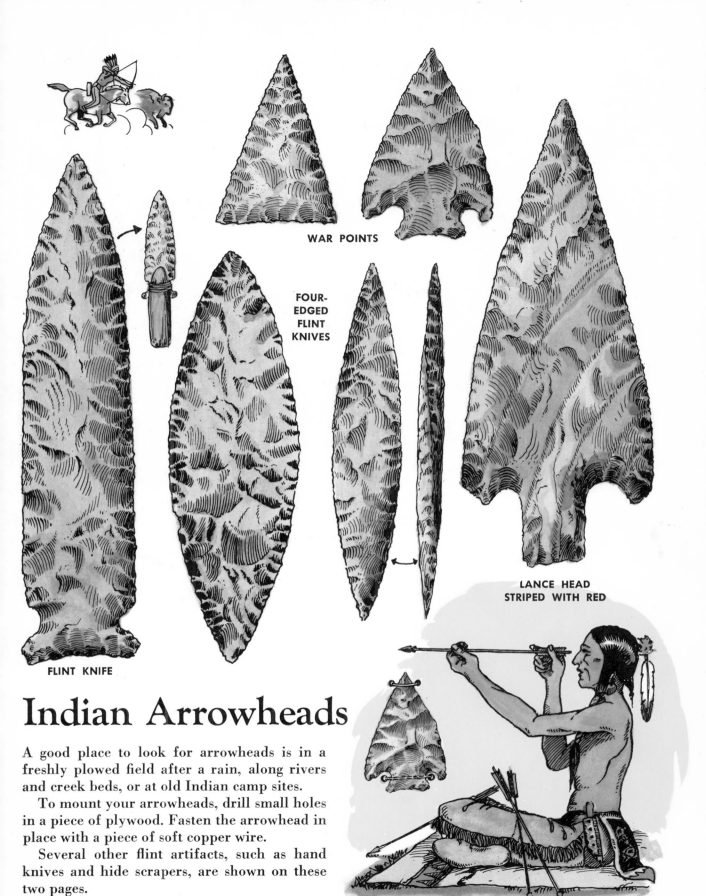

WAR POINTS

FOUR-
EDGED
FLINT
KNIVES

LANCE HEAD
STRIPED WITH RED

FLINT KNIFE

Indian Arrowheads

A good place to look for arrowheads is in a freshly plowed field after a rain, along rivers and creek beds, or at old Indian camp sites.

To mount your arrowheads, drill small holes in a piece of plywood. Fasten the arrowhead in place with a piece of soft copper wire.

Several other flint artifacts, such as hand knives and hide scrapers, are shown on these two pages.

WOODEN BIRDHOUSES

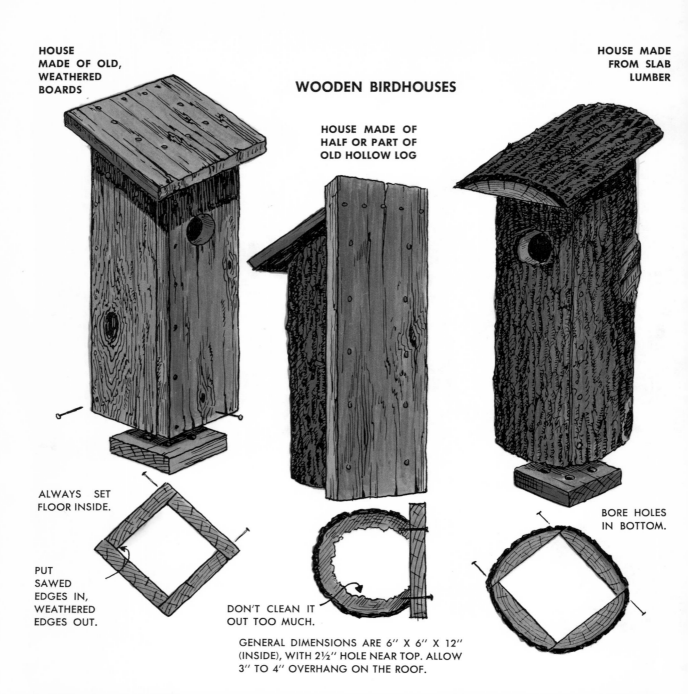

HOUSE MADE OF OLD, WEATHERED BOARDS

HOUSE MADE OF HALF OR PART OF OLD HOLLOW LOG

HOUSE MADE FROM SLAB LUMBER

ALWAYS SET FLOOR INSIDE.

PUT SAWED EDGES IN, WEATHERED EDGES OUT.

DON'T CLEAN IT OUT TOO MUCH.

BORE HOLES IN BOTTOM.

GENERAL DIMENSIONS ARE 6" X 6" X 12" (INSIDE), WITH 2½" HOLE NEAR TOP. ALLOW 3" TO 4" OVERHANG ON THE ROOF.

SIZES FOR BIRDHOUSES

KIND OF BIRD	FLOOR	DEPTH	HOLE	HEIGHT ABOVE GROUND
TITMOUSE	4" x 4"	8"	1¼"	5-12 feet
WREN	4" x 4"	6"-8"	⅞"	6-10 feet
NUTHATCH	4" x 4"	9"	1¼"	12-15 feet
BLUEBIRD	5" x 5"	8"	1½"	5-10 feet
TREE SWALLOW	5" x 5"	6"	1½"	10-15 feet
MARTIN	6" x 6"	6"	1½"	16-20 feet
WOODPECKER	6" x 6"	12"-15"	1½"	12-20 feet
FLICKER	6" x 6"	12"-15"	1½"	8-10 feet
SCREECH OWL	8" x 8"	12"-15"	3"	10-20 feet

Birdhouses

Birds seem to like best the rustic type of house, made from a section of an old hollow log or large limb. The hollow log house in the picture has hung outside of my cabin for many years and there has never been a time when it was not occupied by some bird or animal.

Put birdhouses up as soon as they are completed. They will protect the birds in winter as well as in summer. Put several out in the woods around your camp, and you will soon be pleasantly surprised at the number of tenants attracted to them. Whenever possible, place the house so that the opening faces east or south to keep out the rain and snow.

I haven't seen any birds around with tape measures, but they are rather fussy about the sizes of the interiors and of the openings to their houses. A few birdhouse sizes are listed on page 18.

AN OLD TELEPHONE POLE WITH 1½" HOLES BORED FOR STARTERS WILL GIVE WOODPECKERS SOMETHING TO DO. POLES SHOULD BE 15' HIGH.

Birdhouses (*continued*)

There is a marked increase in the shortage of birdhouses each year, in spite of all the houses that are made and put up. One reason is that more and more land is being cleared of trees all the time. Also when old trees die, they are cut down and hauled away, instead of being left to provide homes for owls, jays, woodpeckers, and wrens.

Another reason for this great shortage of birdhouses is that many of the birdhouses built do not suit the birds. Either the wood is too new, the paint is too fresh, the openings are too large or too small for the particular bird, the entrance perch is not correct, the house is placed too high from or too low to the ground, or offers no protection from cats.

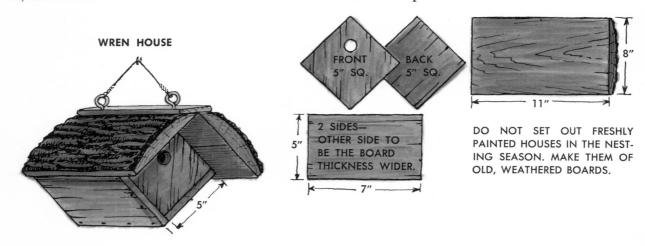

WREN HOUSE

FRONT 5" SQ.

BACK 5" SQ.

2 SIDES— OTHER SIDE TO BE THE BOARD THICKNESS WIDER.

5"

7"

8"

11"

DO NOT SET OUT FRESHLY PAINTED HOUSES IN THE NESTING SEASON. MAKE THEM OF OLD, WEATHERED BOARDS.

5"

BUILDING BIRDHOUSES IS A GOOD TROOP PROJECT, ESPECIALLY WHEN THE BOARDS CAN ALL BE CUT TO SIZE ON A POWER SAW.

BIRDHOUSES OF ROOFING PAPER

IT IS SOMETIMES EASIER TO GET SLATE-COVERED ROOFING PAPER OR STRIP SHINGLES THAN LUMBER. HOUSES LIKE THESE CAN BE MADE EASILY AND QUICKLY, AND WILL LAST LONGER THAN HOUSES MADE ENTIRELY OF WOOD. DIAGRAM AT RIGHT SHOWS DIMENSIONS OF SHINGLES USED FOR THESE BIRDHOUSES. IT ALSO SHOWS HOW WREN HOUSE (BELOW) IS CUT OUT.

36"

21"

12"

7"

7"

HANG ON A LIMB AT LEAST A FOOT OR MORE FROM THE TREE TRUNK.

WREN HOUSE

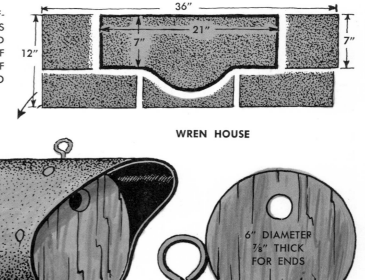

6" DIAMETER 7/8" THICK FOR ENDS

1½" LAP

PUT ONE NAIL AT EACH END.

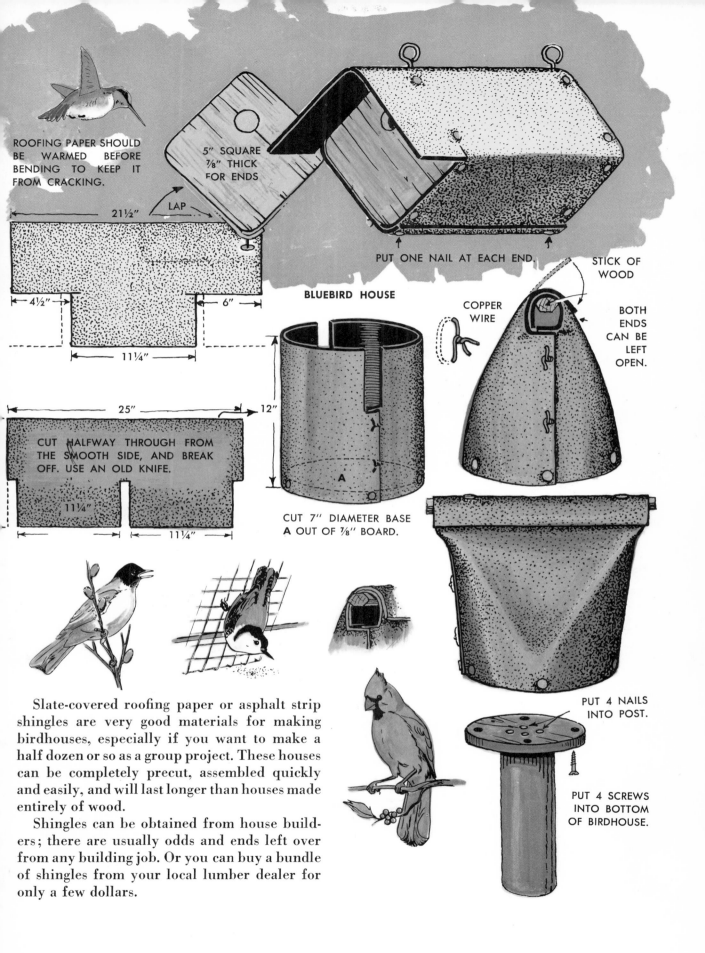

ROOFING PAPER SHOULD BE WARMED BEFORE BENDING TO KEEP IT FROM CRACKING.

5" SQUARE 7/8" THICK FOR ENDS

LAP

21½"

4½"   6"

11¼"

PUT ONE NAIL AT EACH END.

BLUEBIRD HOUSE

COPPER WIRE

STICK OF WOOD

BOTH ENDS CAN BE LEFT OPEN.

25"

12"

CUT HALFWAY THROUGH FROM THE SMOOTH SIDE, AND BREAK OFF. USE AN OLD KNIFE.

11¼"

11¼"

CUT 7" DIAMETER BASE A OUT OF 7/8" BOARD.

PUT 4 NAILS INTO POST.

PUT 4 SCREWS INTO BOTTOM OF BIRDHOUSE.

Slate-covered roofing paper or asphalt strip shingles are very good materials for making birdhouses, especially if you want to make a half dozen or so as a group project. These houses can be completely precut, assembled quickly and easily, and will last longer than houses made entirely of wood.

Shingles can be obtained from house builders; there are usually odds and ends left over from any building job. Or you can buy a bundle of shingles from your local lumber dealer for only a few dollars.

Bird Feeders

You will enjoy standing at your window after a heavy snowfall and watching the birds eat at the feeder you have made for them.

Set up your feeder early, starting with a little food sometime during October. In this way the birds will become acquainted with your feeder and soon will be visiting it regularly. Remember, the birds will depend on you to feed them all winter long, so don't start feeding them unless you intend to continue doing so.

Keep a record of all the different kinds of birds that come to your feeder.

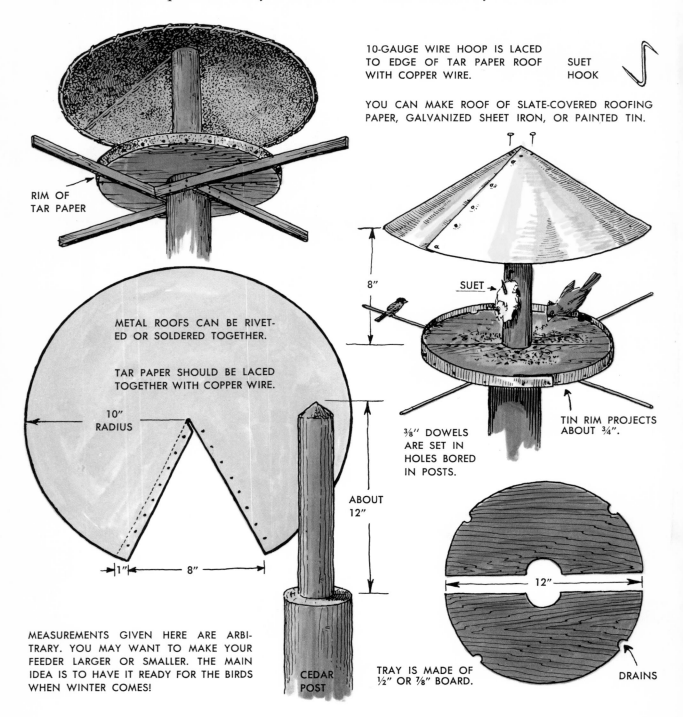

RIM OF TAR PAPER

10-GAUGE WIRE HOOP IS LACED TO EDGE OF TAR PAPER ROOF WITH COPPER WIRE. SUET HOOK

YOU CAN MAKE ROOF OF SLATE-COVERED ROOFING PAPER, GALVANIZED SHEET IRON, OR PAINTED TIN.

METAL ROOFS CAN BE RIVETED OR SOLDERED TOGETHER.

TAR PAPER SHOULD BE LACED TOGETHER WITH COPPER WIRE.

10" RADIUS

1"   8"

SUET

8"

³⁄₈" DOWELS ARE SET IN HOLES BORED IN POSTS.

TIN RIM PROJECTS ABOUT ¾".

ABOUT 12"

CEDAR POST

12"

TRAY IS MADE OF ½" OR ⅞" BOARD.

DRAINS

MEASUREMENTS GIVEN HERE ARE ARBITRARY. YOU MAY WANT TO MAKE YOUR FEEDER LARGER OR SMALLER. THE MAIN IDEA IS TO HAVE IT READY FOR THE BIRDS WHEN WINTER COMES!

JUNCOS ALSO LIKE THESE FEEDERS.

3'

4'   5'

THIS IS A COMBINATION SHELTER-FEEDER WHICH SHOULD BE SET OUT AWAY FROM THE HOUSE, ALONG A WOODED HEDGE, WHERE THERE ARE PHEASANTS, PARTRIDGE, OR QUAIL. WHEN THE GROUND IS COVERED WITH SNOW, BE SURE TO KEEP THIS FEEDER SUPPLIED WITH COARSE SAND, AS ALL BIRDS REQUIRE SAND OR STONES TO DIGEST THEIR FOOD.

AN OLD PIECE OF CANVAS PLACED OVER THE STICKS WILL HELP TO KEEP FEED DRY IN WET WEATHER. COVER CANVAS WITH BRUSH OR CORN STALKS, USING TWINE OR WIRE TO TIE IN PLACE, AS SHOWN.

ROCKS →

Here is a list of the foods I put out in my feeder for birds that live in my locality. This list will differ, of course, if you live in another part of the country.

KIND OF BIRD	SUET	PEANUT BUTTER & NUT MEATS	BREAD CRUMBS, COOKIES, CEREALS	SUNFLOWER SEEDS	PIECES OF ORANGE, APPLE, ETC.	MIXED BIRD FEEDS, CRACKED CORN
BLUE JAY	X	X	X	X		X
CARDINAL		X	X	X		X
CHICKADEE	X	X	X	X		
DOWNY WOODPECKER	X	X	X		X	
EVENING GROSBEAK		X		X		
FIELD SPARROW			X			
FOX SPARROW		X	X			X
HAIRY WOODPECKER	X				X	X
JUNCO			X			X
MOCKINGBIRD					X	X
NUTHATCH	X			X		
PHEASANT				X		X
ROBIN	X		X		X	
SONG SPARROW			X			X
TREE SPARROW		X	X			X

Bird Feeders (*continued*)

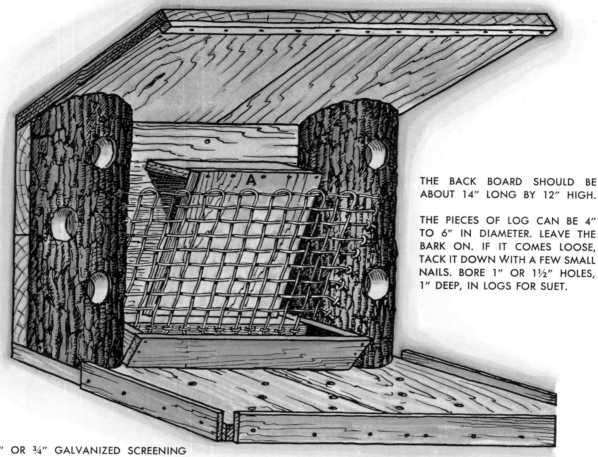

THE BACK BOARD SHOULD BE ABOUT 14" LONG BY 12" HIGH.

THE PIECES OF LOG CAN BE 4" TO 6" IN DIAMETER. LEAVE THE BARK ON. IF IT COMES LOOSE, TACK IT DOWN WITH A FEW SMALL NAILS. BORE 1" OR 1½" HOLES, 1" DEEP, IN LOGS FOR SUET.

USE ½" OR ¾" GALVANIZED SCREENING FOR BREAD HOLDER. FASTEN ENDS WITH SMALL STAPLES.

FEEDER READY TO BE STOCKED

FASTEN FEEDER TO TREE TRUNK OR TO AN OUTSIDE WALL. FILL TROUGH WITH FEED AND SAND. TRY TO HAVE SUET WARM WHEN YOU PACK IT INTO HOLES, OR IT WILL CRUMBLE.

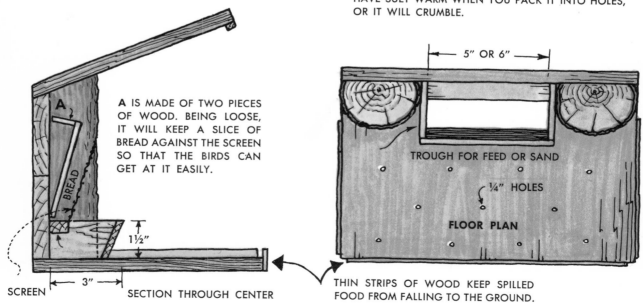

A IS MADE OF TWO PIECES OF WOOD. BEING LOOSE, IT WILL KEEP A SLICE OF BREAD AGAINST THE SCREEN SO THAT THE BIRDS CAN GET AT IT EASILY.

BREAD

1½"

SCREEN

3"

SECTION THROUGH CENTER

5" OR 6"

TROUGH FOR FEED OR SAND

¼" HOLES

FLOOR PLAN

THIN STRIPS OF WOOD KEEP SPILLED FOOD FROM FALLING TO THE GROUND.

TWO EASY-TO-MAKE FEEDERS
TO HANG FROM BRANCHES

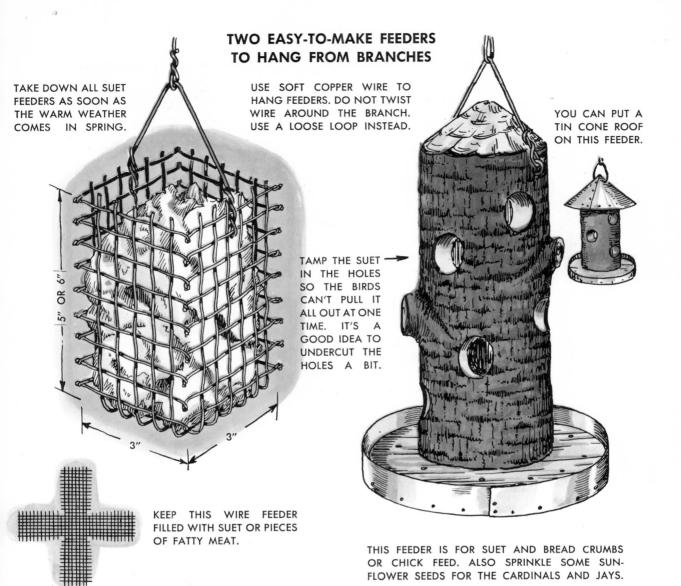

TAKE DOWN ALL SUET FEEDERS AS SOON AS THE WARM WEATHER COMES IN SPRING.

USE SOFT COPPER WIRE TO HANG FEEDERS. DO NOT TWIST WIRE AROUND THE BRANCH. USE A LOOSE LOOP INSTEAD.

YOU CAN PUT A TIN CONE ROOF ON THIS FEEDER.

TAMP THE SUET IN THE HOLES SO THE BIRDS CAN'T PULL IT ALL OUT AT ONE TIME. IT'S A GOOD IDEA TO UNDERCUT THE HOLES A BIT.

5" OR 6"

3"   3"

KEEP THIS WIRE FEEDER FILLED WITH SUET OR PIECES OF FATTY MEAT.

THIS FEEDER IS FOR SUET AND BREAD CRUMBS OR CHICK FEED. ALSO SPRINKLE SOME SUN-FLOWER SEEDS FOR THE CARDINALS AND JAYS.

You can buy sunflower seeds from your local feed supply store or pet shop. If you have a garden, plant your own sunflower seeds?

The sunflower, with its enormous orange-yellow flowers, is a very amazing plant, sometimes growing over 10 feet tall. The center of this huge flower contains hundreds of seeds. In the fall cut off the dried flower heads and shell out the seeds. Or, if you wish, fasten the whole sunflower seed pod on your feeder and the birds will have a great deal of fun picking out the seeds for themselves.

Your local butcher will supply you with suet, and he probably won't even charge you for it when he knows that you are going to use it in a feeder.

I like to make a mixture of bird seeds, nuts, grit, and sunflower seeds combined with melted suet, which I call "bird chop suet":

Melt some suet in a double boiler. (If suet gets too hot, it smokes, so avoid putting it directly over flame.)

To make suet cakes, arrange 6 or 8 paper cups on a tray. In each cup put a large spoonful of the seed mixture. Pour over this mixture a little of the melted suet. Set the tray in a cool place. When the suet has hardened, repeat the process until the cup is filled.

When last layer is hardened, peel off the paper cups and set the cakes of "bird chop suet" in your feeder.

Nature Observation Cage

This is a fine way to observe closely many small animals, reptiles, and large bugs.

The glass front gives you a clear view, and the screened bottom keeps the cage clean.

Some wildlife will not survive in captivity very long, so ask your scoutmaster, science teacher, or a naturalist which animals are the easiest to care for and feed.

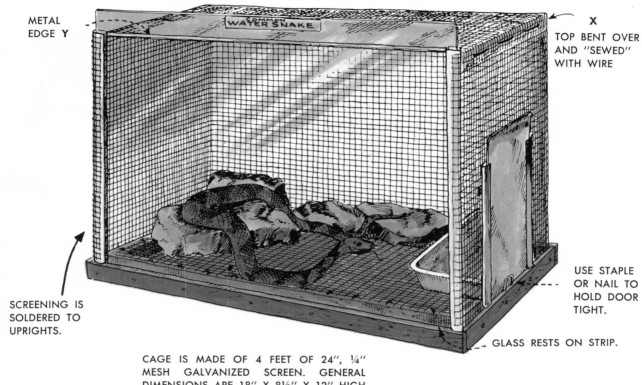

METAL EDGE **Y**

COMMON WATER SNAKE

X TOP BENT OVER AND "SEWED" WITH WIRE

SCREENING IS SOLDERED TO UPRIGHTS.

USE STAPLE OR NAIL TO HOLD DOOR TIGHT.

GLASS RESTS ON STRIP.

CAGE IS MADE OF 4 FEET OF 24", ¼" MESH GALVANIZED SCREEN. GENERAL DIMENSIONS ARE 18" X 8½" X 12" HIGH WITH 12" X 18" GLASS IN FRONT.

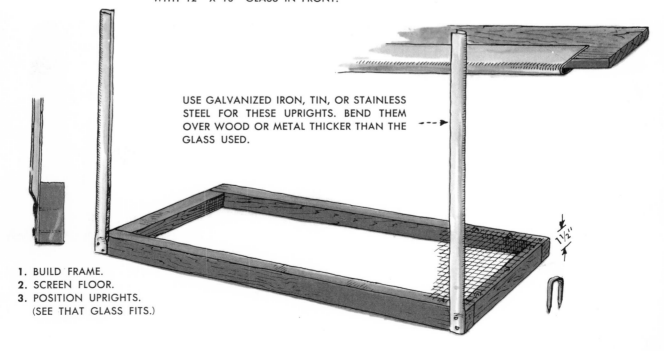

USE GALVANIZED IRON, TIN, OR STAINLESS STEEL FOR THESE UPRIGHTS. BEND THEM OVER WOOD OR METAL THICKER THAN THE GLASS USED.

1½"

1. BUILD FRAME.
2. SCREEN FLOOR.
3. POSITION UPRIGHTS.
   (SEE THAT GLASS FITS.)

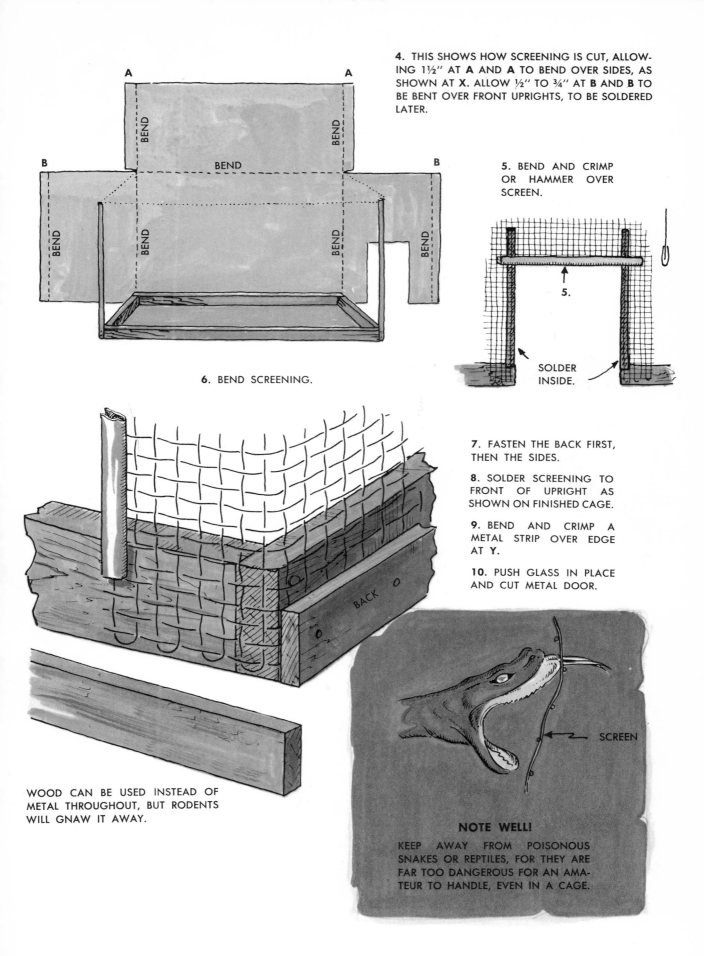

4. THIS SHOWS HOW SCREENING IS CUT, ALLOWING 1½″ AT **A** AND **A** TO BEND OVER SIDES, AS SHOWN AT **X**. ALLOW ½″ TO ¾″ AT **B** AND **B** TO BE BENT OVER FRONT UPRIGHTS, TO BE SOLDERED LATER.

A

A

BEND

BEND

BEND

BEND

B

B

BEND

BEND

BEND

BEND

5. BEND AND CRIMP OR HAMMER OVER SCREEN.

5.

SOLDER INSIDE.

6. BEND SCREENING.

BACK

7. FASTEN THE BACK FIRST, THEN THE SIDES.

8. SOLDER SCREENING TO FRONT OF UPRIGHT AS SHOWN ON FINISHED CAGE.

9. BEND AND CRIMP A METAL STRIP OVER EDGE AT **Y**.

10. PUSH GLASS IN PLACE AND CUT METAL DOOR.

WOOD CAN BE USED INSTEAD OF METAL THROUGHOUT, BUT RODENTS WILL GNAW IT AWAY.

SCREEN

NOTE WELL!

KEEP AWAY FROM POISONOUS SNAKES OR REPTILES, FOR THEY ARE FAR TOO DANGEROUS FOR AN AMATEUR TO HANDLE, EVEN IN A CAGE.

BIRDS ARE MAN'S BEST FRIEND WHEN IT COMES TO KILLING INSECT PESTS.

A PRUNING SHEARS IS BEST FOR CUTTING OFF THE WEBS. EARLY MORNING IS A GOOD TIME TO DESTROY WEBS.

1. CUT OFF THE ENTIRE TENT. BE SURE NOT TO MISS ANY OF IT.

2. THROW THE WEBS INTO A GUNNY SACK. BE SURE SACK HAS NO HOLES, OR WORMS MIGHT ESCAPE.

3. DESTROY GUNNY SACKS BY PLACING THEM OVER A GOOD FIRE. BE CAREFUL NOT TO BURN YOURSELF. DOUSE YOUR FIRE WHEN YOU ARE FINISHED.

YELLOW-BILLED AND BLACK-BILLED CUCKOOS ARE VERY FOND OF TENT CATERPILLARS.

28

Destroying Insect Pests

This is not a hobby or a craft project, but I am including it in this book because it is a service that every boy and girl can give to his or her community.

The tent caterpillar builds its web in the spring, usually in the crotch of a tree. The fall webworm lays its eggs in the summer, and the webs are formed in the fall. Both types of webs house thousands of leaf-destroying insects.

To destroy the webs, you will need a pair of pruning shears, a gunny sack, and some matches. Be careful not to burn yourself. When you are through, water down the area where you made the fire so the flames will not spread.

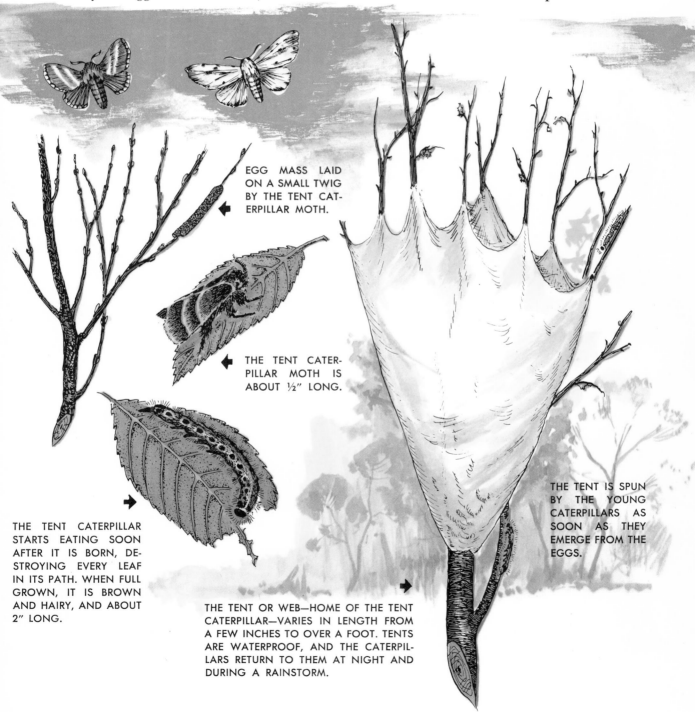

EGG MASS LAID ON A SMALL TWIG BY THE TENT CATERPILLAR MOTH.

THE TENT CATERPILLAR MOTH IS ABOUT ½" LONG.

THE TENT CATERPILLAR STARTS EATING SOON AFTER IT IS BORN, DESTROYING EVERY LEAF IN ITS PATH. WHEN FULL GROWN, IT IS BROWN AND HAIRY, AND ABOUT 2" LONG.

THE TENT OR WEB—HOME OF THE TENT CATERPILLAR—VARIES IN LENGTH FROM A FEW INCHES TO OVER A FOOT. TENTS ARE WATERPROOF, AND THE CATERPILLARS RETURN TO THEM AT NIGHT AND DURING A RAINSTORM.

THE TENT IS SPUN BY THE YOUNG CATERPILLARS AS SOON AS THEY EMERGE FROM THE EGGS.

Indian Hair Ornaments

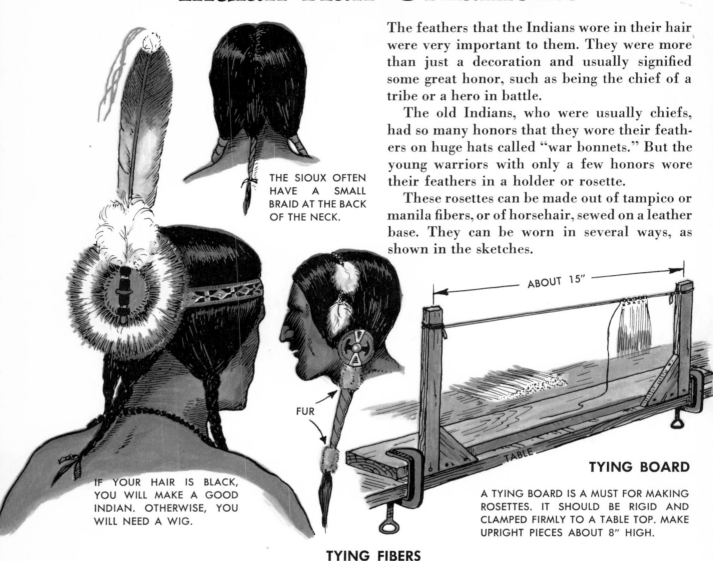

THE SIOUX OFTEN HAVE A SMALL BRAID AT THE BACK OF THE NECK.

IF YOUR HAIR IS BLACK, YOU WILL MAKE A GOOD INDIAN. OTHERWISE, YOU WILL NEED A WIG.

FUR

The feathers that the Indians wore in their hair were very important to them. They were more than just a decoration and usually signified some great honor, such as being the chief of a tribe or a hero in battle.

The old Indians, who were usually chiefs, had so many honors that they wore their feathers on huge hats called "war bonnets." But the young warriors with only a few honors wore their feathers in a holder or rosette.

These rosettes can be made out of tampico or manila fibers, or of horsehair, sewed on a leather base. They can be worn in several ways, as shown in the sketches.

ABOUT 15"

TABLE

TYING BOARD

A TYING BOARD IS A MUST FOR MAKING ROSETTES. IT SHOULD BE RIGID AND CLAMPED FIRMLY TO A TABLE TOP. MAKE UPRIGHT PIECES ABOUT 8" HIGH.

TYING FIBERS

1. CORD AND TIE STRING SHOULD BE WELL WAXED. USE A SOFT CORD FOR THE BASE AND LINEN THREAD FOR TYING. TAKE ABOUT 12 OR 14 STRANDS, 7" LONG, TO A BUNCH. TIE THEM UNIFORMLY, WORKING FROM RIGHT TO LEFT.

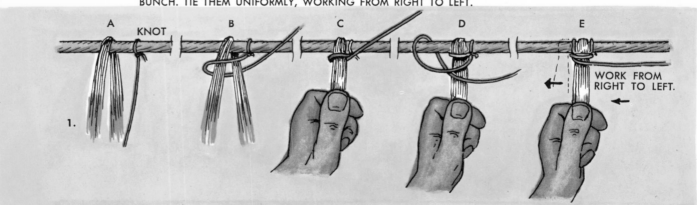

1.   A   KNOT   B   C   D   E

WORK FROM RIGHT TO LEFT.

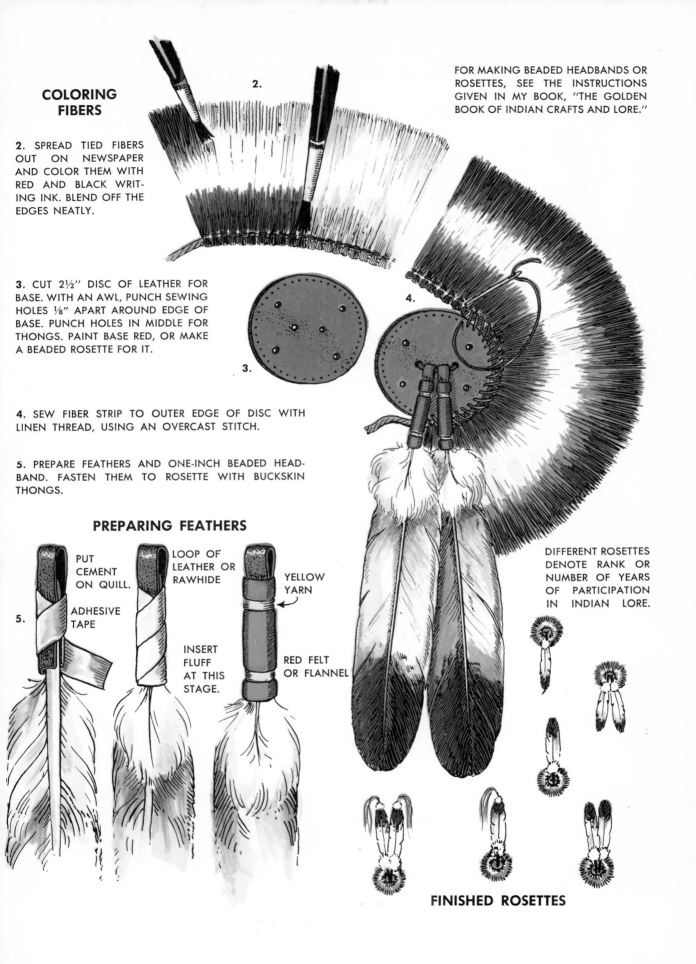

COLORING FIBERS

2. SPREAD TIED FIBERS OUT ON NEWSPAPER AND COLOR THEM WITH RED AND BLACK WRITING INK. BLEND OFF THE EDGES NEATLY.

3. CUT 2½" DISC OF LEATHER FOR BASE. WITH AN AWL, PUNCH SEWING HOLES ⅛" APART AROUND EDGE OF BASE. PUNCH HOLES IN MIDDLE FOR THONGS. PAINT BASE RED, OR MAKE A BEADED ROSETTE FOR IT.

4. SEW FIBER STRIP TO OUTER EDGE OF DISC WITH LINEN THREAD, USING AN OVERCAST STITCH.

5. PREPARE FEATHERS AND ONE-INCH BEADED HEADBAND. FASTEN THEM TO ROSETTE WITH BUCKSKIN THONGS.

PREPARING FEATHERS

PUT CEMENT ON QUILL.

ADHESIVE TAPE

LOOP OF LEATHER OR RAWHIDE

INSERT FLUFF AT THIS STAGE.

YELLOW YARN

RED FELT OR FLANNEL

FOR MAKING BEADED HEADBANDS OR ROSETTES, SEE THE INSTRUCTIONS GIVEN IN MY BOOK, "THE GOLDEN BOOK OF INDIAN CRAFTS AND LORE."

DIFFERENT ROSETTES DENOTE RANK OR NUMBER OF YEARS OF PARTICIPATION IN INDIAN LORE.

FINISHED ROSETTES

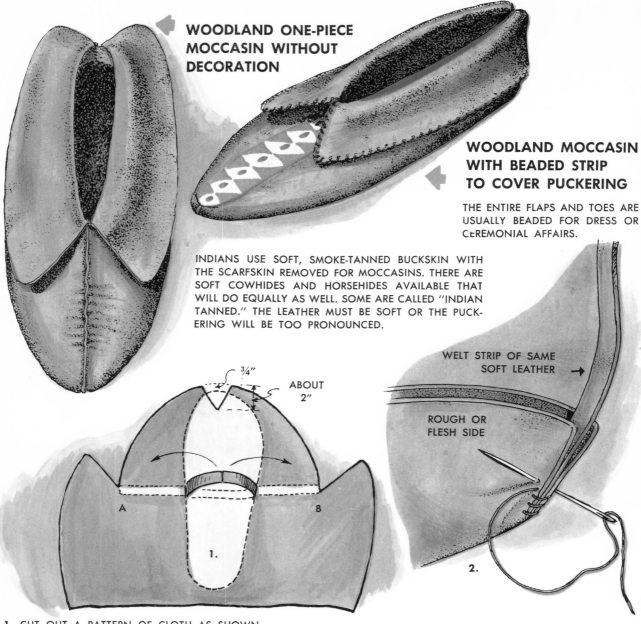

WOODLAND ONE-PIECE MOCCASIN WITHOUT DECORATION

WOODLAND MOCCASIN WITH BEADED STRIP TO COVER PUCKERING

THE ENTIRE FLAPS AND TOES ARE USUALLY BEADED FOR DRESS OR CEREMONIAL AFFAIRS.

INDIANS USE SOFT, SMOKE-TANNED BUCKSKIN WITH THE SCARFSKIN REMOVED FOR MOCCASINS. THERE ARE SOFT COWHIDES AND HORSEHIDES AVAILABLE THAT WILL DO EQUALLY AS WELL. SOME ARE CALLED "INDIAN TANNED." THE LEATHER MUST BE SOFT OR THE PUCKERING WILL BE TOO PRONOUNCED.

WELT STRIP OF SAME SOFT LEATHER

ROUGH OR FLESH SIDE

3/4"

ABOUT 2"

A   B

1.

2.

1. CUT OUT A PATTERN OF CLOTH AS SHOWN ABOVE. MEASURE AROUND INSTEP TO DETERMINE THE WIDTH FROM "A" TO "B" AND ADD ABOUT ⅛" TO ¼" FOR THE SEAM. THEN FIT THE CLOTH PATTERN FOR SIZE AND SHAPE.

THERE ARE NO LEFTS AND RIGHTS, BUT THE MOC-CASINS WILL GRADUALLY SHAPE THEMSELVES TO YOUR FEET.

2. INSERT A WELT STRIP AND SEW AS SHOWN, USING A GLOVER'S TRIANGULAR POINTED NEEDLE AND A GOOD WAXED THREAD.

3. SEW ENTIRE TOE, TAKING IN OR PUCKERING AS YOU GO ALONG, TO FLATTEN THE TOE.

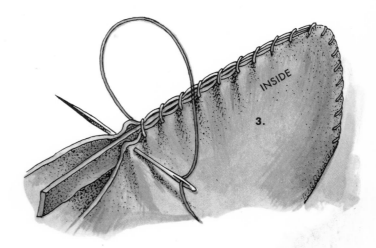

INSIDE

3.

Woodland Moccasins

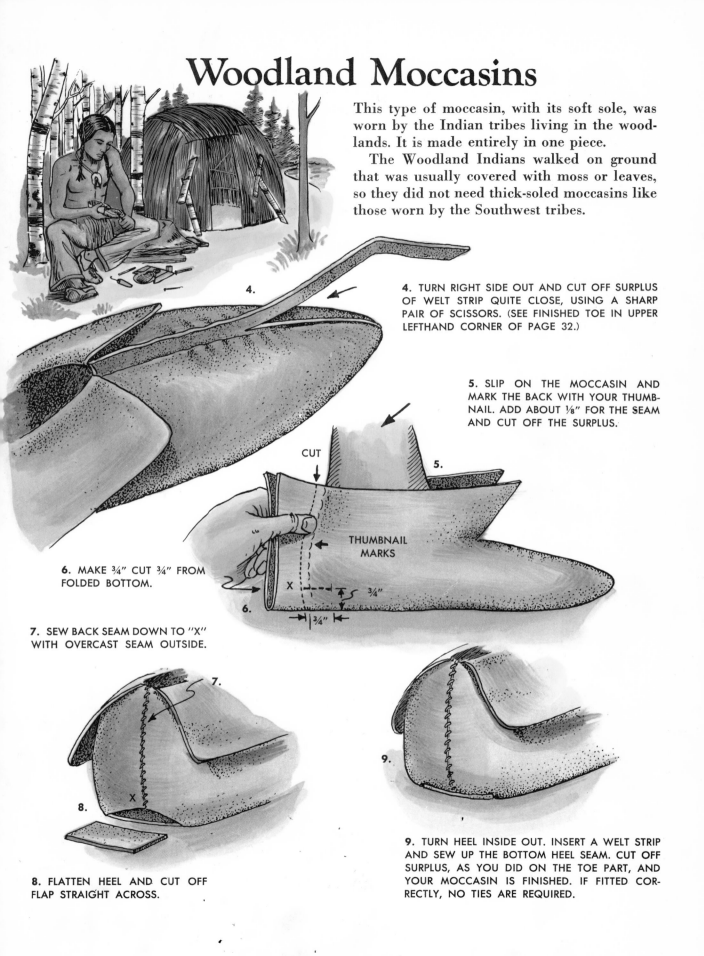

This type of moccasin, with its soft sole, was worn by the Indian tribes living in the woodlands. It is made entirely in one piece.

The Woodland Indians walked on ground that was usually covered with moss or leaves, so they did not need thick-soled moccasins like those worn by the Southwest tribes.

4. TURN RIGHT SIDE OUT AND CUT OFF SURPLUS OF WELT STRIP QUITE CLOSE, USING A SHARP PAIR OF SCISSORS. (SEE FINISHED TOE IN UPPER LEFTHAND CORNER OF PAGE 32.)

5. SLIP ON THE MOCCASIN AND MARK THE BACK WITH YOUR THUMBNAIL. ADD ABOUT ⅛" FOR THE SEAM AND CUT OFF THE SURPLUS.

CUT

THUMBNAIL MARKS

X

¾"

¾"

6. MAKE ¾" CUT ¾" FROM FOLDED BOTTOM.

7. SEW BACK SEAM DOWN TO "X" WITH OVERCAST SEAM OUTSIDE.

X

8. FLATTEN HEEL AND CUT OFF FLAP STRAIGHT ACROSS.

9. TURN HEEL INSIDE OUT. INSERT A WELT STRIP AND SEW UP THE BOTTOM HEEL SEAM. CUT OFF SURPLUS, AS YOU DID ON THE TOE PART, AND YOUR MOCCASIN IS FINISHED. IF FITTED CORRECTLY, NO TIES ARE REQUIRED.

Beaded Capes

Beaded capes of various designs were worn by the Indians of many tribes. They are, no doubt, variations of the white man's vest, or the vestments worn by the early missionaries.

They are very colorful and, as a rule, are worn without a shirt. For dancing, they are much more comfortable than a full shirt.

Capes can be made from either buckskin or colored broadcloth or blanket cloth. Make a pattern before cutting into your good material.

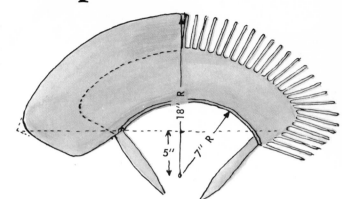

MODOC

THIS CAPE IS MADE OUT OF ONE BUCKSKIN WITH A SIMPLE BORDER OF PONY BEADS. NOTE HOW EVERY OTHER FRINGE HAS BEEN CUT OUT. BIND THE NECK WITH BIAS TAPE AND SEW ON THE TIES. TIES MAY BE THE SAME COLOR AS THE TAPE.

CHEYENNE

THIS CAPE IS MADE OF BROADCLOTH OR BLANKET CLOTH WITH A BUCKSKIN COLLAR. THE BEADED BORDER IS OF CONTRASTING COLORS. ALMOST ANY KIND OF FRINGE MAY BE USED. THIS ONE IS OF 1¼" OR 1½" TIN CONES AND LARGE NECKLACE BEADS. THE BUFFALO IS SOLID BEADWORK. THE BACK IS SHAPED LIKE FRONT.

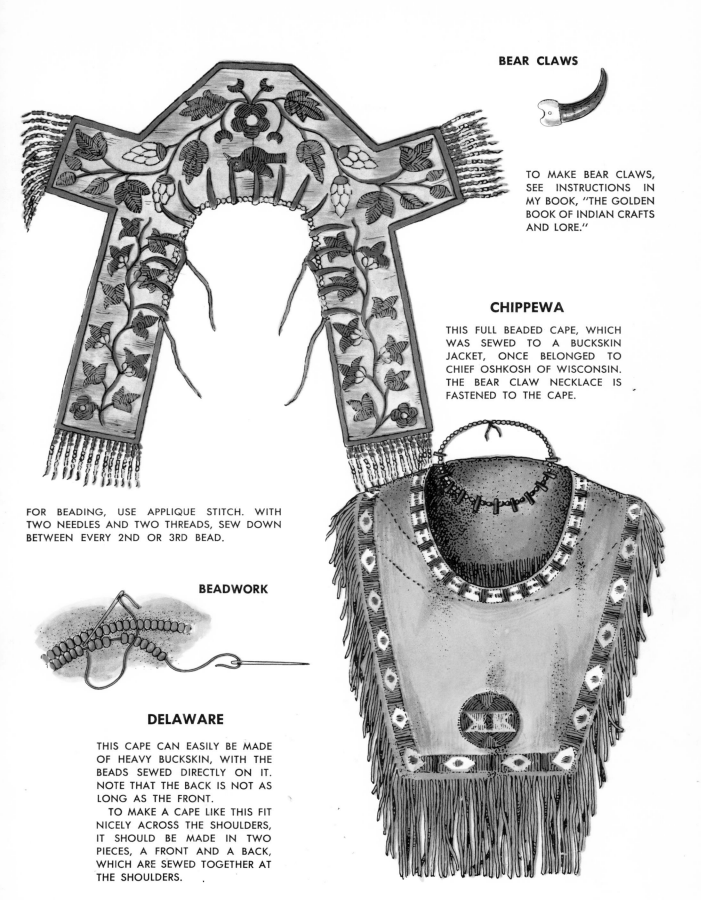

BEAR CLAWS

TO MAKE BEAR CLAWS, SEE INSTRUCTIONS IN MY BOOK, "THE GOLDEN BOOK OF INDIAN CRAFTS AND LORE."

CHIPPEWA

THIS FULL BEADED CAPE, WHICH WAS SEWED TO A BUCKSKIN JACKET, ONCE BELONGED TO CHIEF OSHKOSH OF WISCONSIN. THE BEAR CLAW NECKLACE IS FASTENED TO THE CAPE.

FOR BEADING, USE APPLIQUE STITCH. WITH TWO NEEDLES AND TWO THREADS, SEW DOWN BETWEEN EVERY 2ND OR 3RD BEAD.

BEADWORK

DELAWARE

THIS CAPE CAN EASILY BE MADE OF HEAVY BUCKSKIN, WITH THE BEADS SEWED DIRECTLY ON IT. NOTE THAT THE BACK IS NOT AS LONG AS THE FRONT.

TO MAKE A CAPE LIKE THIS FIT NICELY ACROSS THE SHOULDERS, IT SHOULD BE MADE IN TWO PIECES, A FRONT AND A BACK, WHICH ARE SEWED TOGETHER AT THE SHOULDERS.

Bead Necklaces

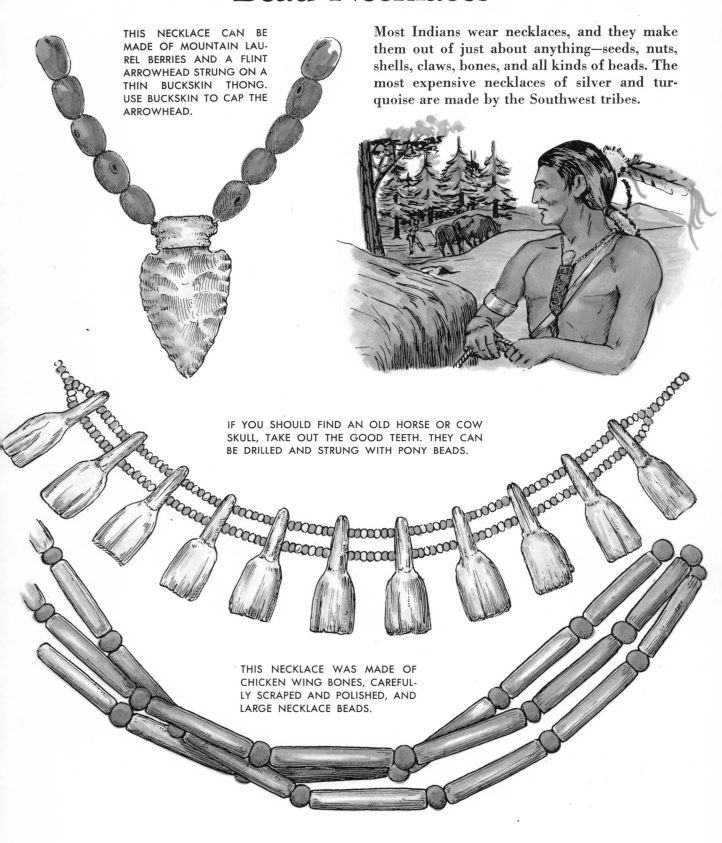

THIS NECKLACE CAN BE MADE OF MOUNTAIN LAUREL BERRIES AND A FLINT ARROWHEAD STRUNG ON A THIN BUCKSKIN THONG. USE BUCKSKIN TO CAP THE ARROWHEAD.

Most Indians wear necklaces, and they make them out of just about anything—seeds, nuts, shells, claws, bones, and all kinds of beads. The most expensive necklaces of silver and turquoise are made by the Southwest tribes.

IF YOU SHOULD FIND AN OLD HORSE OR COW SKULL, TAKE OUT THE GOOD TEETH. THEY CAN BE DRILLED AND STRUNG WITH PONY BEADS.

THIS NECKLACE WAS MADE OF CHICKEN WING BONES, CAREFULLY SCRAPED AND POLISHED, AND LARGE NECKLACE BEADS.

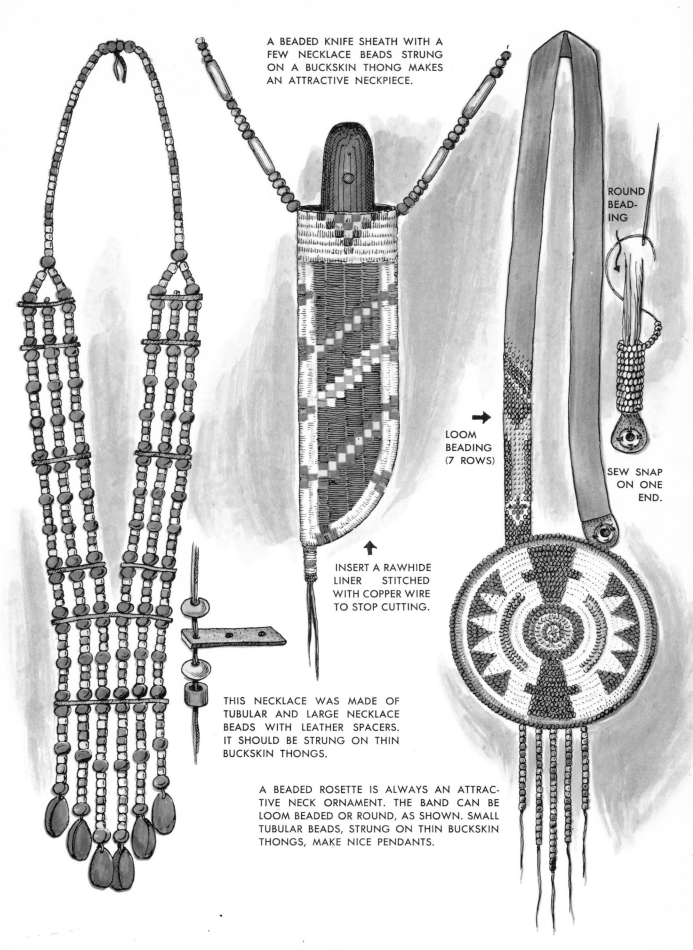

A BEADED KNIFE SHEATH WITH A FEW NECKLACE BEADS STRUNG ON A BUCKSKIN THONG MAKES AN ATTRACTIVE NECKPIECE.

ROUND BEADING

LOOM BEADING (7 ROWS)

SEW SNAP ON ONE END.

INSERT A RAWHIDE LINER STITCHED WITH COPPER WIRE TO STOP CUTTING.

THIS NECKLACE WAS MADE OF TUBULAR AND LARGE NECKLACE BEADS WITH LEATHER SPACERS. IT SHOULD BE STRUNG ON THIN BUCKSKIN THONGS.

A BEADED ROSETTE IS ALWAYS AN ATTRACTIVE NECK ORNAMENT. THE BAND CAN BE LOOM BEADED OR ROUND, AS SHOWN. SMALL TUBULAR BEADS, STRUNG ON THIN BUCKSKIN THONGS, MAKE NICE PENDANTS.

37

Feathered Fans

The Indians prized the feathers of the Bald Eagle for their war bonnets because the eagle stood for strength and courage. The feathers of owls, wild turkeys, herons, woodpeckers, and many smaller birds were also used for adornments.

The Pueblos and tribes living in Virginia raised eagles and turkeys in captivity for their supply of feathers. The feathers were pulled out of the wings and tails of these birds with no discomfort to them, and in a short time they grew new feathers.

The big problem in making a fan is securing the feathers, since many states protect birds. A butcher or a farmer may be able to help you out with goose and turkey feathers.

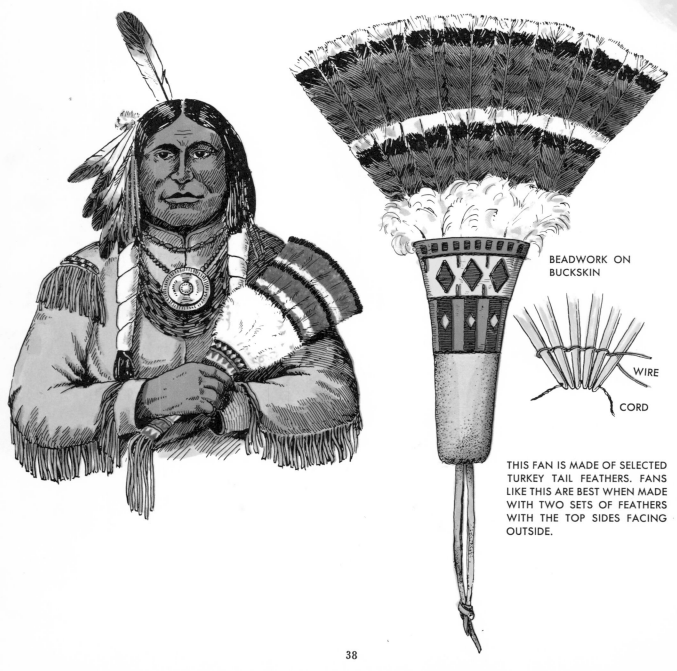

BEADWORK ON BUCKSKIN

WIRE

CORD

THIS FAN IS MADE OF SELECTED TURKEY TAIL FEATHERS. FANS LIKE THIS ARE BEST WHEN MADE WITH TWO SETS OF FEATHERS WITH THE TOP SIDES FACING OUTSIDE.

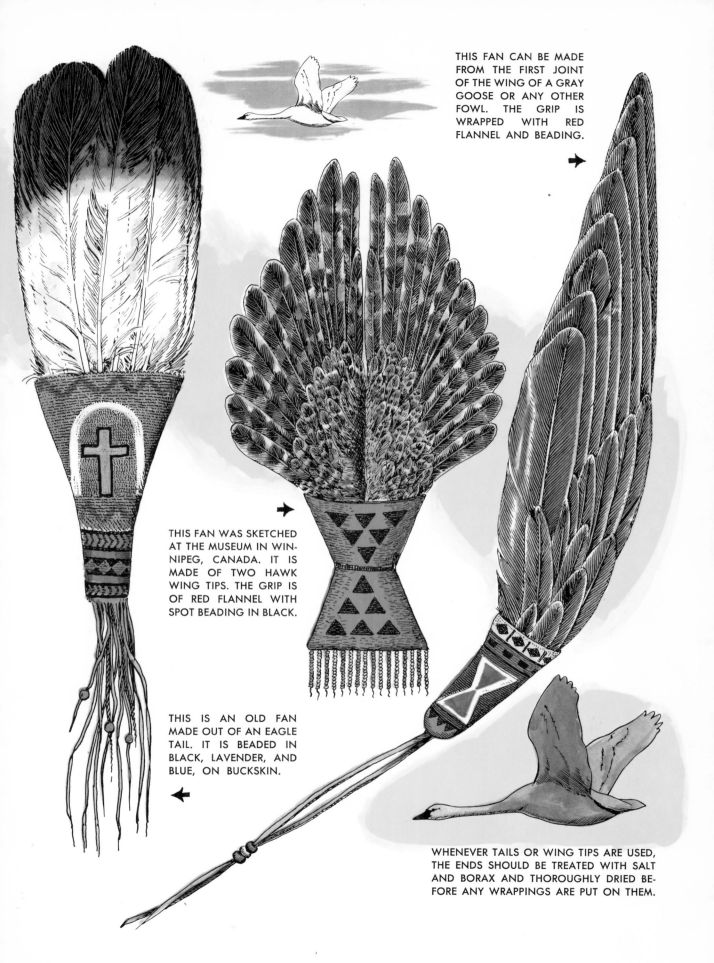

THIS FAN CAN BE MADE FROM THE FIRST JOINT OF THE WING OF A GRAY GOOSE OR ANY OTHER FOWL. THE GRIP IS WRAPPED WITH RED FLANNEL AND BEADING.

THIS FAN WAS SKETCHED AT THE MUSEUM IN WINNIPEG, CANADA. IT IS MADE OF TWO HAWK WING TIPS. THE GRIP IS OF RED FLANNEL WITH SPOT BEADING IN BLACK.

THIS IS AN OLD FAN MADE OUT OF AN EAGLE TAIL. IT IS BEADED IN BLACK, LAVENDER, AND BLUE, ON BUCKSKIN.

WHENEVER TAILS OR WING TIPS ARE USED, THE ENDS SHOULD BE TREATED WITH SALT AND BORAX AND THOROUGHLY DRIED BEFORE ANY WRAPPINGS ARE PUT ON THEM.

Turtle-shell Rattles

Because turtles are found in practically every part of the North American continent, it is natural that many Indian tribes used their shells for rattles.

Rattles made from small shells—4 to 5 inches in diameter—did not have handles, but were fastened to the legs with a buckskin thong. As the Indian moved or danced about, the rattles kept up a steady clatter.

Indian tribes usually considered the turtle rattles sacred and used them only for important ceremonial occasions. Your rattle will make a dandy Indian decoration for your room. You will also want to use it at Indian lore ceremonies. To clack it, keep time to the drum beat with a single quick movement of the hand, or move it quickly back and forth with the drum beat to produce a rattlesnake-like buzz.

BOX TURTLE RATTLE

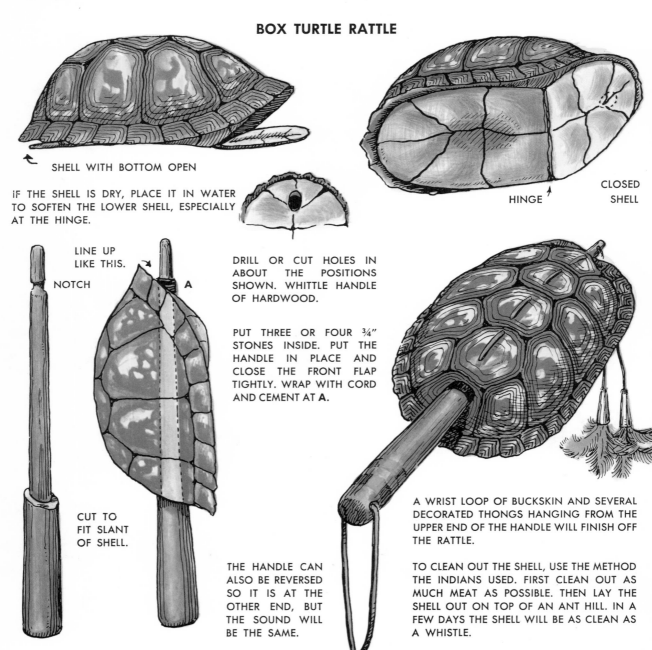

SHELL WITH BOTTOM OPEN

IF THE SHELL IS DRY, PLACE IT IN WATER TO SOFTEN THE LOWER SHELL, ESPECIALLY AT THE HINGE.

HINGE   CLOSED SHELL

LINE UP LIKE THIS.

NOTCH   A

DRILL OR CUT HOLES IN ABOUT THE POSITIONS SHOWN. WHITTLE HANDLE OF HARDWOOD.

PUT THREE OR FOUR ¾" STONES INSIDE. PUT THE HANDLE IN PLACE AND CLOSE THE FRONT FLAP TIGHTLY. WRAP WITH CORD AND CEMENT AT A.

CUT TO FIT SLANT OF SHELL.

THE HANDLE CAN ALSO BE REVERSED SO IT IS AT THE OTHER END, BUT THE SOUND WILL BE THE SAME.

A WRIST LOOP OF BUCKSKIN AND SEVERAL DECORATED THONGS HANGING FROM THE UPPER END OF THE HANDLE WILL FINISH OFF THE RATTLE.

TO CLEAN OUT THE SHELL, USE THE METHOD THE INDIANS USED. FIRST CLEAN OUT AS MUCH MEAT AS POSSIBLE. THEN LAY THE SHELL OUT ON TOP OF AN ANT HILL. IN A FEW DAYS THE SHELL WILL BE AS CLEAN AS A WHISTLE.

MUD TURTLE RATTLE

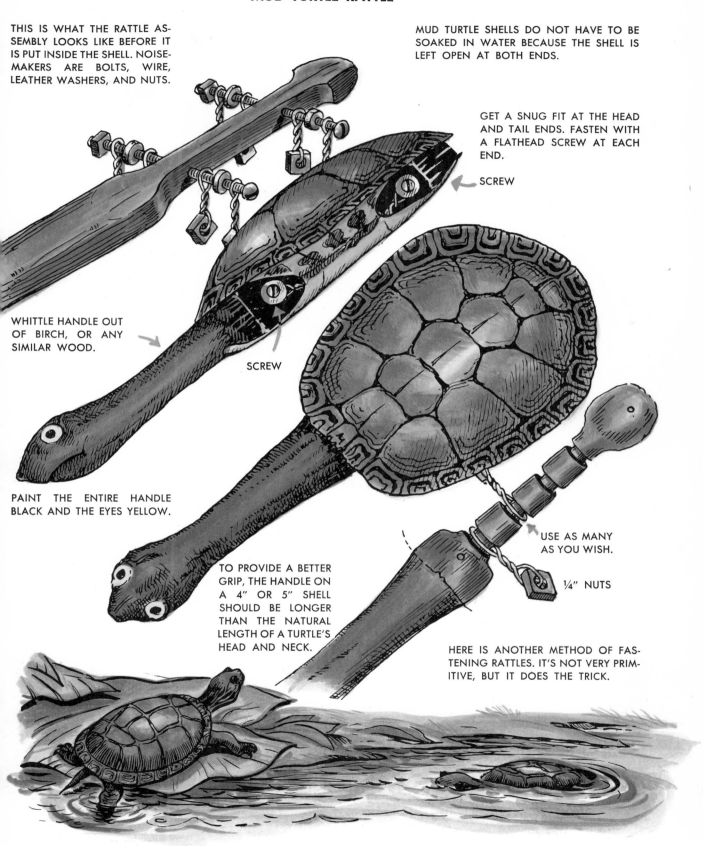

THIS IS WHAT THE RATTLE AS-
SEMBLY LOOKS LIKE BEFORE IT
IS PUT INSIDE THE SHELL. NOISE-
MAKERS ARE BOLTS, WIRE,
LEATHER WASHERS, AND NUTS.

MUD TURTLE SHELLS DO NOT HAVE TO BE
SOAKED IN WATER BECAUSE THE SHELL IS
LEFT OPEN AT BOTH ENDS.

GET A SNUG FIT AT THE HEAD
AND TAIL ENDS. FASTEN WITH
A FLATHEAD SCREW AT EACH
END.

SCREW

WHITTLE HANDLE OUT
OF BIRCH, OR ANY
SIMILAR WOOD.

SCREW

PAINT THE ENTIRE HANDLE
BLACK AND THE EYES YELLOW.

TO PROVIDE A BETTER
GRIP, THE HANDLE ON
A 4" OR 5" SHELL
SHOULD BE LONGER
THAN THE NATURAL
LENGTH OF A TURTLE'S
HEAD AND NECK.

USE AS MANY
AS YOU WISH.

¼" NUTS

HERE IS ANOTHER METHOD OF FAS-
TENING RATTLES. IT'S NOT VERY PRIM-
ITIVE, BUT IT DOES THE TRICK.

41

ANTELOPE MAN

LARGE FOXTAIL

RED YARN

SNAKE MEN

Hopi Snake Dance

In late August, on alternating years, the Hopi Indians of Arizona put on their famous Snake Dance ceremony. This dance, sometimes known as the Rain Dance, is celebrated as a prayer for rain. The Hopi believe that the snakes used in this ceremony are the children of the Snake Hero and the Snake Maiden, and that they have the power to make rain clouds gather and rain fall. The snakes used are two species of rattlesnake—the bull and the whipsnake—neither of which is particularly venomous.

The dance is performed by the members of the Snake and Antelope Fraternities. These two fraternities meet in separate Kivas, or underground clubrooms.

The ceremony takes nine days, and during the first four days the snakes are gathered by the priests from the four directions of the compass. Sacred corn meal or sand is sprinkled on the snakes, which is said to temporarily blind them, and the priests handle them with apparently no ill effects.

On the ninth day, the Antelope priests, dressed in the traditional costumes for the Snake Dance, march out of their Kiva—each with a turtle-shell rattle fastened to his knee. They march around the plaza four times. Then each priest stamps on a small board, after which they form a line on each side of the dance area. This tells the underground gods that the ceremony has begun. The dance is accompanied by a low chant that gradually increases in volume, and the line sways back and forth in a circular motion. After the ceremony, the snakes are carried back to the four points of the compass by the priests and released.

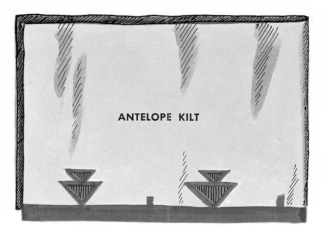

ANTELOPE KILT

SNAKE KILT

WRAP-AROUND KILTS ARE MADE OF 8-OZ. CANVAS, 45" X 20", PAINTED WITH REGULAR HOUSE PAINT.
EACH DRAWING SHOWS HALF OF A KILT. USE LARGE SAFETY PINS TO FASTEN KILT AT WAIST.

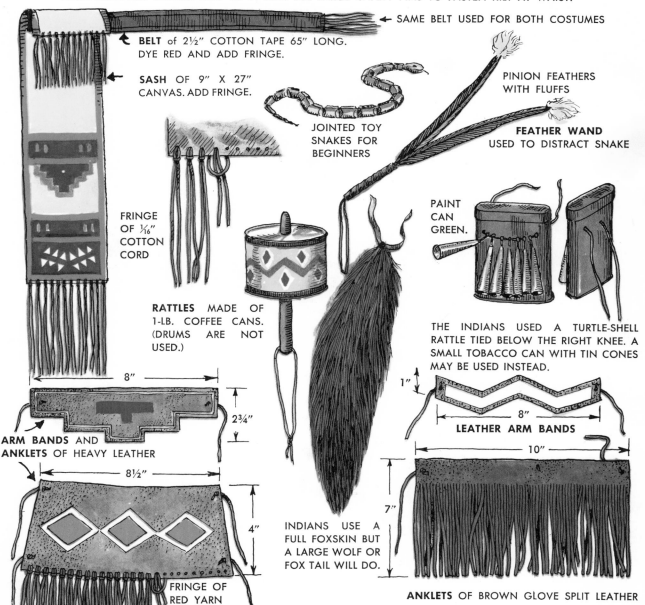

← SAME BELT USED FOR BOTH COSTUMES

BELT of 2½" COTTON TAPE 65" LONG.
DYE RED AND ADD FRINGE.

SASH of 9" X 27"
CANVAS. ADD FRINGE.

JOINTED TOY
SNAKES FOR
BEGINNERS

PINION FEATHERS
WITH FLUFFS

FEATHER WAND
USED TO DISTRACT SNAKE

FRINGE
OF 1/16"
COTTON
CORD

PAINT
CAN
GREEN.

RATTLES MADE OF
1-LB. COFFEE CANS.
(DRUMS ARE NOT
USED.)

THE INDIANS USED A TURTLE-SHELL
RATTLE TIED BELOW THE RIGHT KNEE. A
SMALL TOBACCO CAN WITH TIN CONES
MAY BE USED INSTEAD.

8"

2¾"

1"

8"

LEATHER ARM BANDS

ARM BANDS AND
ANKLETS OF HEAVY LEATHER

10"

8½"

4"

7"

INDIANS USE A
FULL FOXSKIN BUT
A LARGE WOLF OR
FOX TAIL WILL DO.

FRINGE OF
RED YARN

ANKLETS OF BROWN GLOVE SPLIT LEATHER

KWAHU KACHINA DOLL

THE HOPIS USE COTTONWOOD ROOTS FOR THEIR DOLLS, BUT YOU CAN USE WHITE PINE OR BASS-WOOD. SQUARE UP THE DRAWINGS BELOW, AS SHOWN, TO GET THE CORRECT PROPORTIONS. PERHAPS YOU CAN WORK DIRECTLY FROM THE DRAWINGS WITHOUT ENLARGING THEM. FOR THE BODY, YOU'LL NEED A BLOCK OF WOOD 2½" X 3" X 8".

AFTER WHITTLING THE BODY, MAKE THE ARMS AND GLUE THEM ON. NEXT CUT OUT THE FOXSKIN, THE TAIL, AND THE SASH. GLUE AND TACK THEM ON THE BODY IN THAT ORDER. CUT THE WINGS OUT OF ⅛" WOOD. THEN ADD THE EYES, EARS, AND BEAK. PAINT THE DOLL AS SHOWN HERE, BUT DO NOT VARNISH OR LACQUER IT. ADD FEATHERS, AND YOU'RE ALL SET.

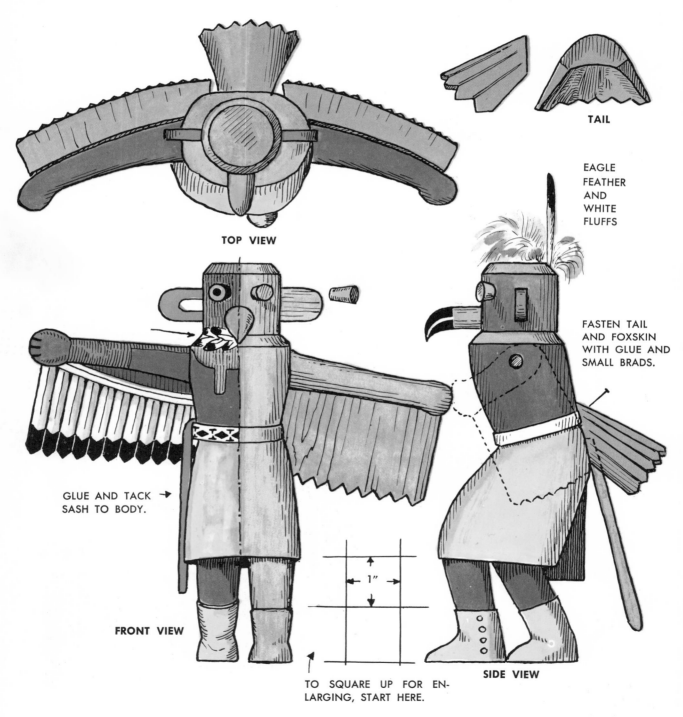

TOP VIEW

TAIL

EAGLE FEATHER AND WHITE FLUFFS

FASTEN TAIL AND FOXSKIN WITH GLUE AND SMALL BRADS.

GLUE AND TACK → SASH TO BODY.

FRONT VIEW

1"

TO SQUARE UP FOR ENLARGING, START HERE.

SIDE VIEW

Hopi Kachina Dolls

The Hopi Indians believe in many gods rather than in one great spirit. They also believe in supernatural beings called Kachinas, who form a link between man and his gods.

In the spring of the year the Kachinas supposedly come from their homes in the San Francisco mountains to visit the pueblos. At this time, the Hopis have very colorful religious ceremonies, some of which are held out-of-doors, with Indian men masked and painted to represent the Kachinas. During the "Nimon" ceremony on the last day, tiny Kachina dolls are given out to the children. These dolls have been carved out of cottonwood during the winter months by the Hopi men.

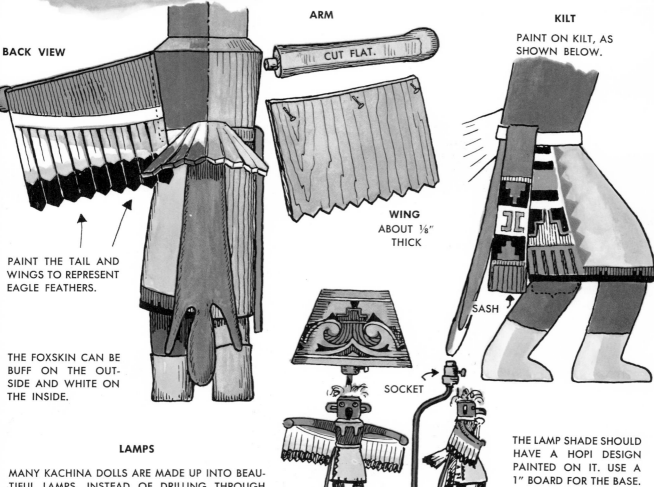

BACK VIEW

ARM

CUT FLAT.

KILT

PAINT ON KILT, AS SHOWN BELOW.

PAINT THE TAIL AND WINGS TO REPRESENT EAGLE FEATHERS.

WING
ABOUT ⅛"
THICK

SASH

THE FOXSKIN CAN BE BUFF ON THE OUTSIDE AND WHITE ON THE INSIDE.

SOCKET

LAMPS

MANY KACHINA DOLLS ARE MADE UP INTO BEAUTIFUL LAMPS. INSTEAD OF DRILLING THROUGH THE DOLL FOR WIRING, BEND A ⅜" POLISHED BRASS TUBE, AS SHOWN AT RIGHT. FASTEN IT INTO A WOODEN BASE.

THE LAMP SHADE SHOULD HAVE A HOPI DESIGN PAINTED ON IT. USE A 1" BOARD FOR THE BASE. IT CAN BE ANY SHAPE.

1. WIND THE STRAP TWO OR THREE TIMES AROUND THE GROOVE IN THE TOP.

2. SET IT DOWN ON HARD GROUND OR FLOOR, AND GIVE THE STRAP A QUICK PULL TO START THE TOP.

MAKE THE WHIP OUT OF A 3-FT. LENGTH OF ½" BRANCH. TIE A LEATHER STRAP, ABOUT ¼" WIDE AND 8" OR 10" LONG, TO THE END OF IT.

3. FLICK THE TOP WITH THE WHIP TO KEEP IT SPINNING.

TOPS MADE OF HARDWOOD ARE EASIER TO KEEP SPINNING.

Hopi Whipping Tops

The Hopi Indian children, like children the world over, love toys. During the winter months the men of the tribe carve tiny Kachina dolls for the girls, and little bows and arrows for the boys. These toys are made of cottonwood and are given to the children during the Kachina festival in the spring.

Another toy that the Hopi boys and girls are especially fond of is the whipping top. These tops are whittled out of any kind of wood that is available. Indian children have a lot of fun trying to see who can spin his top most skillfully and keep it going the longest.

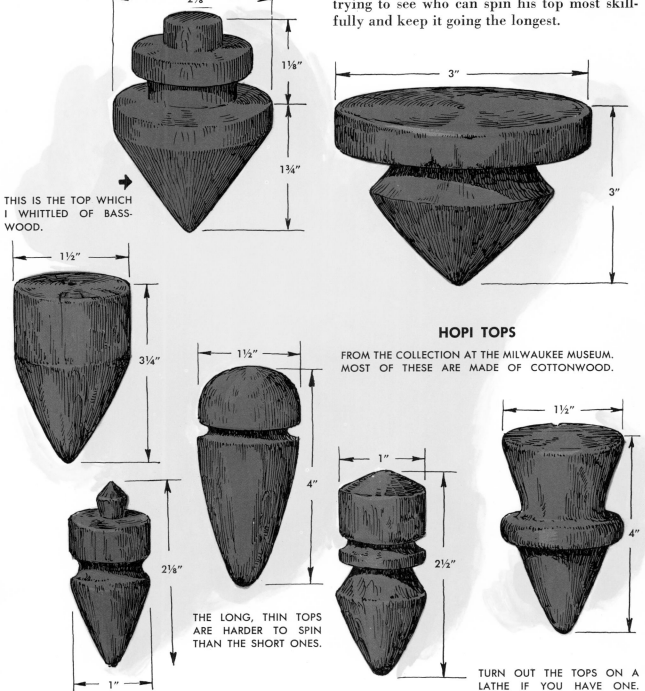

2⅛"
1⅛"
1¾"

THIS IS THE TOP WHICH I WHITTLED OF BASSWOOD.

3"
3"

HOPI TOPS

FROM THE COLLECTION AT THE MILWAUKEE MUSEUM. MOST OF THESE ARE MADE OF COTTONWOOD.

1½"
3¼"

1½"
4"

2⅛"
1"

THE LONG, THIN TOPS ARE HARDER TO SPIN THAN THE SHORT ONES.

1"
2½"

1½"
4"

TURN OUT THE TOPS ON A LATHE IF YOU HAVE ONE.

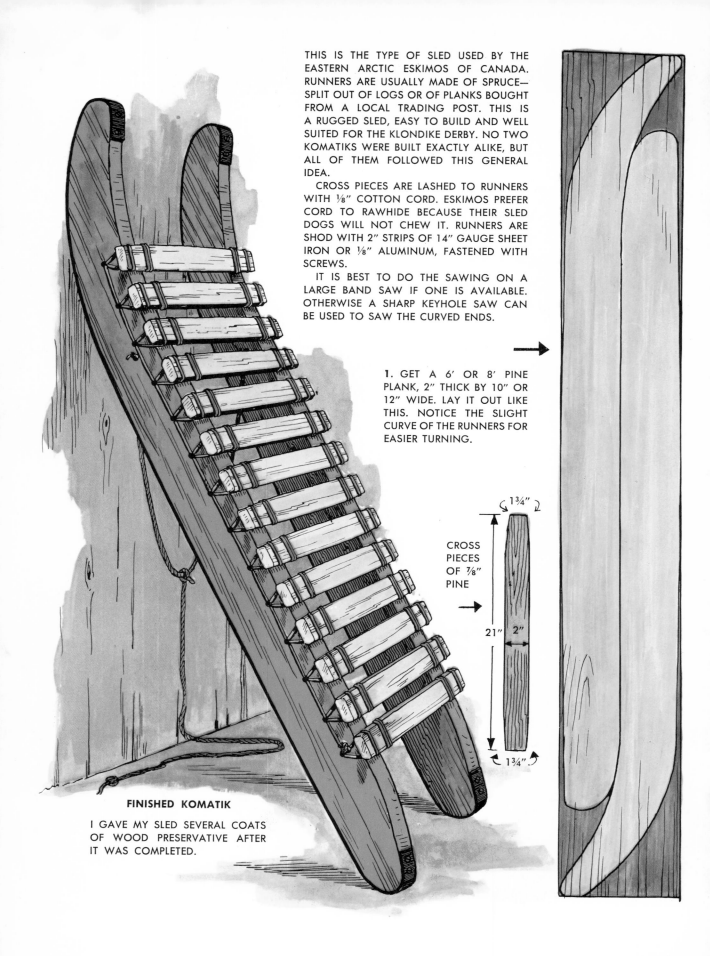

THIS IS THE TYPE OF SLED USED BY THE EASTERN ARCTIC ESKIMOS OF CANADA. RUNNERS ARE USUALLY MADE OF SPRUCE—SPLIT OUT OF LOGS OR OF PLANKS BOUGHT FROM A LOCAL TRADING POST. THIS IS A RUGGED SLED, EASY TO BUILD AND WELL SUITED FOR THE KLONDIKE DERBY. NO TWO KOMATIKS WERE BUILT EXACTLY ALIKE, BUT ALL OF THEM FOLLOWED THIS GENERAL IDEA.

CROSS PIECES ARE LASHED TO RUNNERS WITH ⅛" COTTON CORD. ESKIMOS PREFER CORD TO RAWHIDE BECAUSE THEIR SLED DOGS WILL NOT CHEW IT. RUNNERS ARE SHOD WITH 2" STRIPS OF 14" GAUGE SHEET IRON OR ⅛" ALUMINUM, FASTENED WITH SCREWS.

IT IS BEST TO DO THE SAWING ON A LARGE BAND SAW IF ONE IS AVAILABLE. OTHERWISE A SHARP KEYHOLE SAW CAN BE USED TO SAW THE CURVED ENDS.

1. GET A 6' OR 8' PINE PLANK, 2" THICK BY 10" OR 12" WIDE. LAY IT OUT LIKE THIS. NOTICE THE SLIGHT CURVE OF THE RUNNERS FOR EASIER TURNING.

1¾"

CROSS PIECES OF ⅞" PINE

21"   2"

1¾"

FINISHED KOMATIK

I GAVE MY SLED SEVERAL COATS OF WOOD PRESERVATIVE AFTER IT WAS COMPLETED.

Eskimo Komatik or Sled

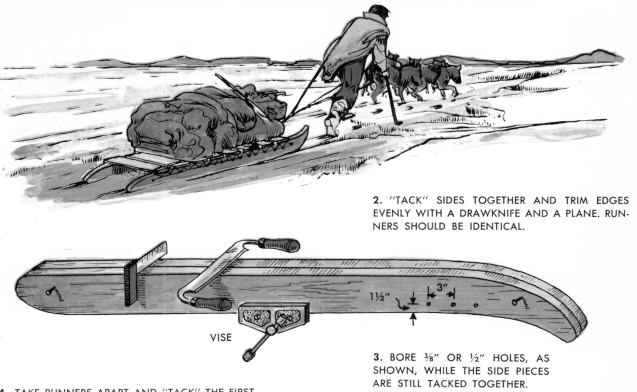

2. "TACK" SIDES TOGETHER AND TRIM EDGES EVENLY WITH A DRAWKNIFE AND A PLANE. RUNNERS SHOULD BE IDENTICAL.

VISE

1½"   3"

3. BORE ⅜" OR ½" HOLES, AS SHOWN, WHILE THE SIDE PIECES ARE STILL TACKED TOGETHER.

4. TAKE RUNNERS APART AND "TACK" THE FIRST AND THE LAST CROSS PIECES IN POSITION. FRONT END OF SLED SHOULD BE SLIGHTLY WIDER THAN THE BACK END.

14"   14½"

5. THE METAL RUNNERS SHOULD BE FASTENED WITH COUNTERSUNK FLATHEAD SCREWS, 6" OR 8" APART.

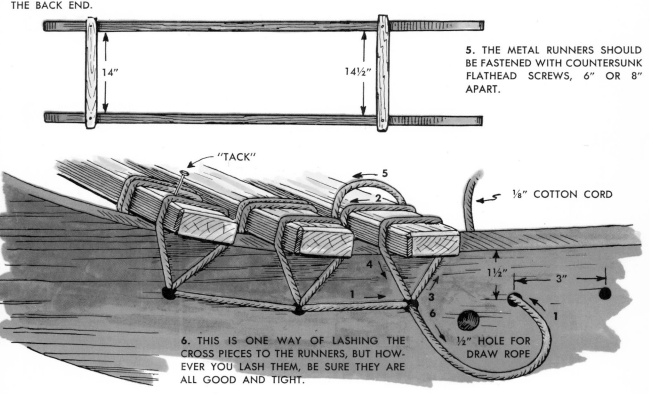

"TACK"

5

2

⅛" COTTON CORD

4

1   3

6

1½"   3"

1

½" HOLE FOR DRAW ROPE

6. THIS IS ONE WAY OF LASHING THE CROSS PIECES TO THE RUNNERS, BUT HOWEVER YOU LASH THEM, BE SURE THEY ARE ALL GOOD AND TIGHT.

Cree Trail Toboggan

The first toboggans that the white men saw in the New World were made by the Algonquian Indians of northeast North America. The name toboggan is said to have come from the Abnaki Indian word, "udaba-gan," meaning "used for dragging."

This project may look difficult, but it is really quite easy. And you will have many years of fun with such a toboggan.

GREEN CEDAR WOULD BE THE IDEAL WOOD TO USE, BUT ½" STRAIGHT-GRAINED BIRCH OR ASH WILL WORK OUT JUST AS WELL.

1. IF USING CEDAR, SPLIT A 10" LOG IN TWO. THEN SPLIT A 1" PLANK FROM EACH HALF WITH WOODEN WEDGES.

2. HEW PLANKS WITH AN AX AND SMOOTH THEM DOWN TO ⅝" WITH A DRAWKNIFE.

OR

IF USING ½" ASH OR BIRCH, ALL YOU HAVE TO DO IS CUT THEM TO SHAPE AND THIN THEM DOWN AT THE BEND.

3. PLACE BOARDS TOGETHER AND MARK WHERE THE CROSS PIECES GO. DRILL HOLES FOR THE COPPER WIRE LASHINGS.

4. TURN OVER AND CUT GROOVES IN BOTTOM FOR WIRE TO SINK INTO.

5. LASH CROSS ARMS WITH SOFT 14-GAUGE COPPER WIRE. PULL WIRE UP TIGHT AND TWIST THE ENDS. CUT OFF SURPLUS AND BEND ENDS OUT OF THE WAY.

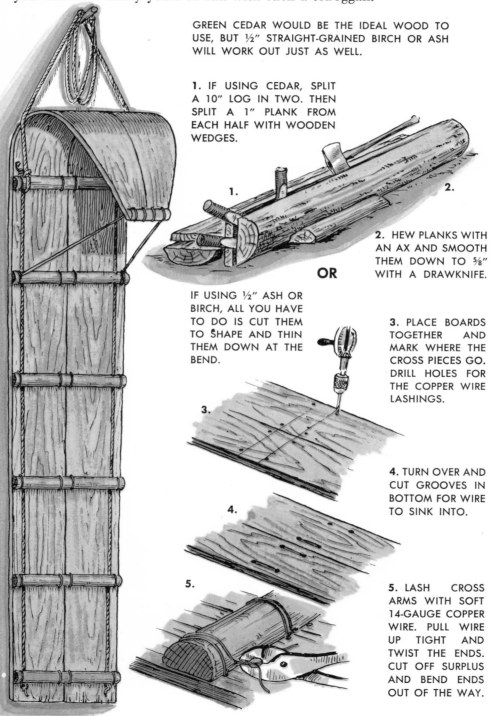

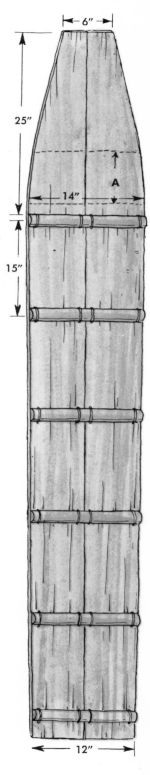

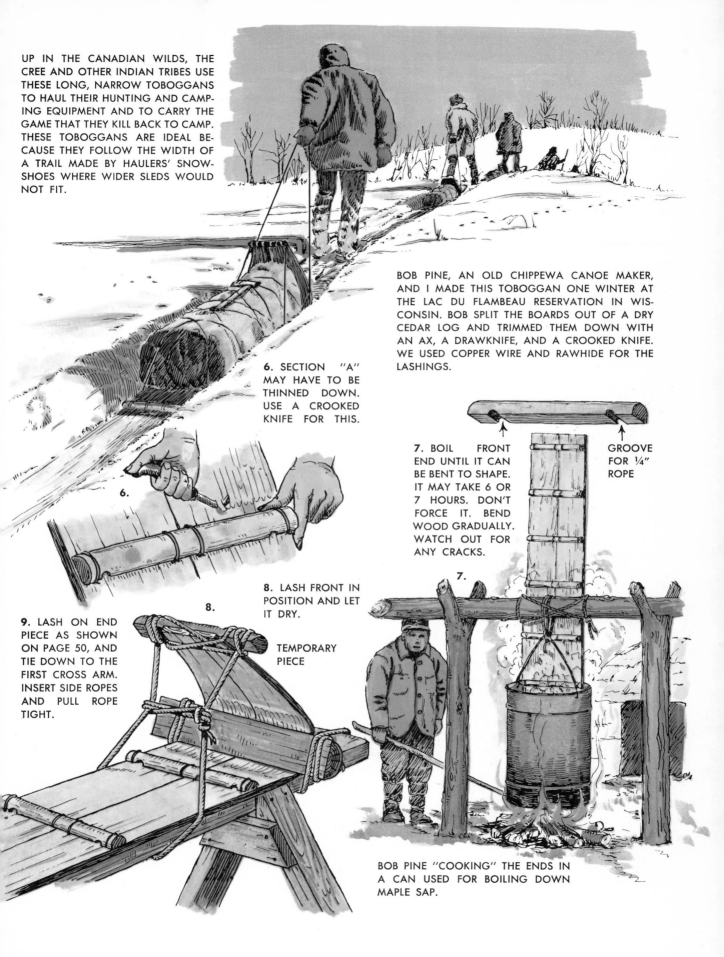

UP IN THE CANADIAN WILDS, THE CREE AND OTHER INDIAN TRIBES USE THESE LONG, NARROW TOBOGGANS TO HAUL THEIR HUNTING AND CAMPING EQUIPMENT AND TO CARRY THE GAME THAT THEY KILL BACK TO CAMP. THESE TOBOGGANS ARE IDEAL BECAUSE THEY FOLLOW THE WIDTH OF A TRAIL MADE BY HAULERS' SNOWSHOES WHERE WIDER SLEDS WOULD NOT FIT.

BOB PINE, AN OLD CHIPPEWA CANOE MAKER, AND I MADE THIS TOBOGGAN ONE WINTER AT THE LAC DU FLAMBEAU RESERVATION IN WISCONSIN. BOB SPLIT THE BOARDS OUT OF A DRY CEDAR LOG AND TRIMMED THEM DOWN WITH AN AX, A DRAWKNIFE, AND A CROOKED KNIFE. WE USED COPPER WIRE AND RAWHIDE FOR THE LASHINGS.

6. SECTION "A" MAY HAVE TO BE THINNED DOWN. USE A CROOKED KNIFE FOR THIS.

6.

7. BOIL FRONT END UNTIL IT CAN BE BENT TO SHAPE. IT MAY TAKE 6 OR 7 HOURS. DON'T FORCE IT. BEND WOOD GRADUALLY. WATCH OUT FOR ANY CRACKS.

GROOVE FOR 1/4" ROPE

7.

8. LASH FRONT IN POSITION AND LET IT DRY.

8.

TEMPORARY PIECE

9. LASH ON END PIECE AS SHOWN ON PAGE 50, AND TIE DOWN TO THE FIRST CROSS ARM. INSERT SIDE ROPES AND PULL ROPE TIGHT.

BOB PINE "COOKING" THE ENDS IN A CAN USED FOR BOILING DOWN MAPLE SAP.

RUNNERS

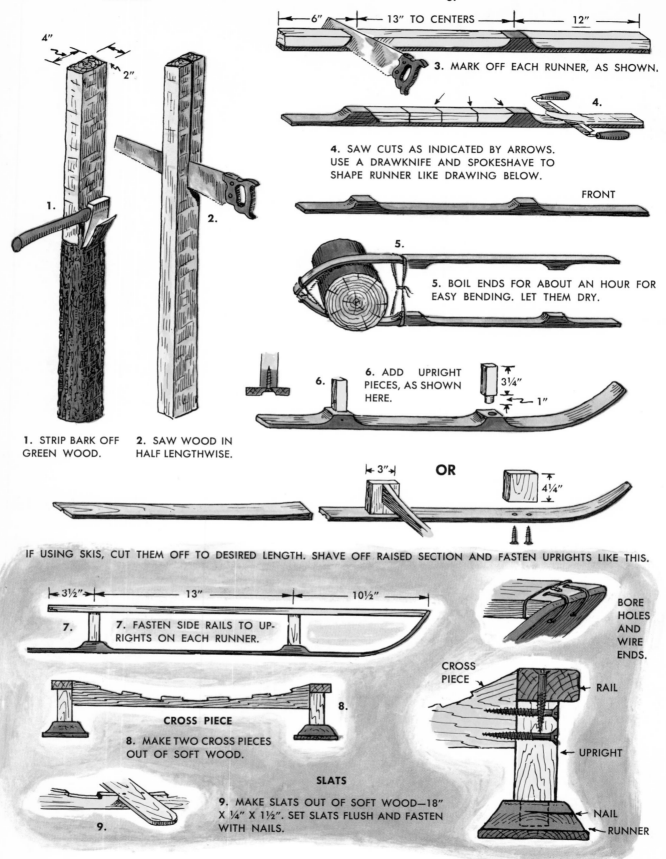

3. MARK OFF EACH RUNNER, AS SHOWN.
6" — 13" TO CENTERS — 12"

4. SAW CUTS AS INDICATED BY ARROWS.
USE A DRAWKNIFE AND SPOKESHAVE TO
SHAPE RUNNER LIKE DRAWING BELOW.

FRONT

5. BOIL ENDS FOR ABOUT AN HOUR FOR
EASY BENDING. LET THEM DRY.

6. ADD UPRIGHT
PIECES, AS SHOWN
HERE.
3¼"
1"

1. STRIP BARK OFF
GREEN WOOD.

2. SAW WOOD IN
HALF LENGTHWISE.

3" **OR** 4¼"

IF USING SKIS, CUT THEM OFF TO DESIRED LENGTH. SHAVE OFF RAISED SECTION AND FASTEN UPRIGHTS LIKE THIS.

3½" — 13" — 10½"

7. FASTEN SIDE RAILS TO UP-
RIGHTS ON EACH RUNNER.

BORE
HOLES
AND
WIRE
ENDS.

CROSS
PIECE

CROSS PIECE

RAIL

8. MAKE TWO CROSS PIECES
OUT OF SOFT WOOD.

UPRIGHT

SLATS

9. MAKE SLATS OUT OF SOFT WOOD—18"
X ¼" X 1½". SET SLATS FLUSH AND FASTEN
WITH NAILS.

NAIL

RUNNER

Pack-rack Sled

This is an especially nice sled for your next winter hike. With a pack like this, when your back begins to ache, all you have to do is reverse the duffle on the rack and pull it along.

This sled is very easy to build, and if you have a pair of old skis to cut down for runners, half the work is done. If not, you can make the runners out of green ash, elm, or hickory. The rest of the sled can be made out of pine or cedar or any other soft, easy-to-cut wood. Use wire or rawhide to hold the ends of the runners to the frame. The straps can be made out of cotton webbing or belt leather.

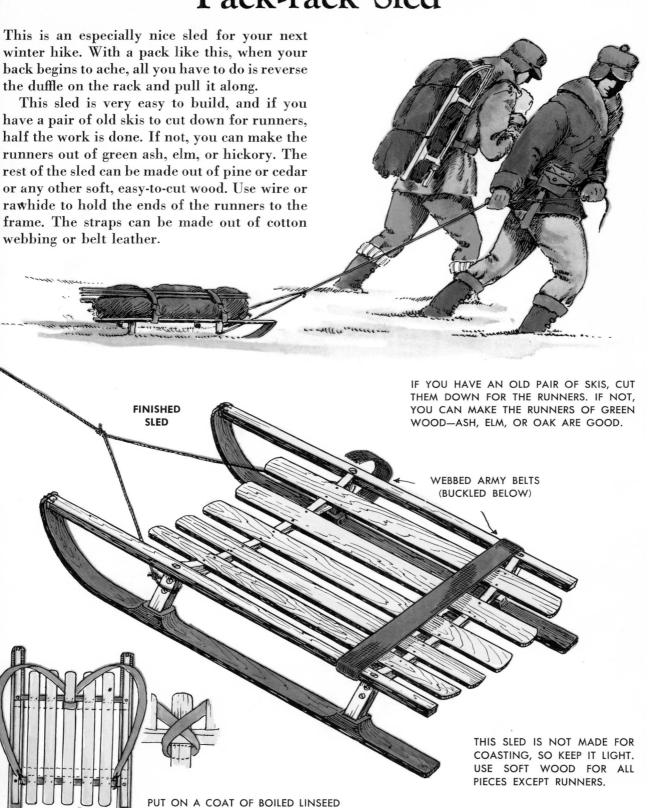

FINISHED SLED

IF YOU HAVE AN OLD PAIR OF SKIS, CUT THEM DOWN FOR THE RUNNERS. IF NOT, YOU CAN MAKE THE RUNNERS OF GREEN WOOD—ASH, ELM, OR OAK ARE GOOD.

WEBBED ARMY BELTS (BUCKLED BELOW)

THIS SLED IS NOT MADE FOR COASTING, SO KEEP IT LIGHT. USE SOFT WOOD FOR ALL PIECES EXCEPT RUNNERS.

PUT ON A COAT OF BOILED LINSEED OIL OR SPAR VARNISH FOR FINISH.

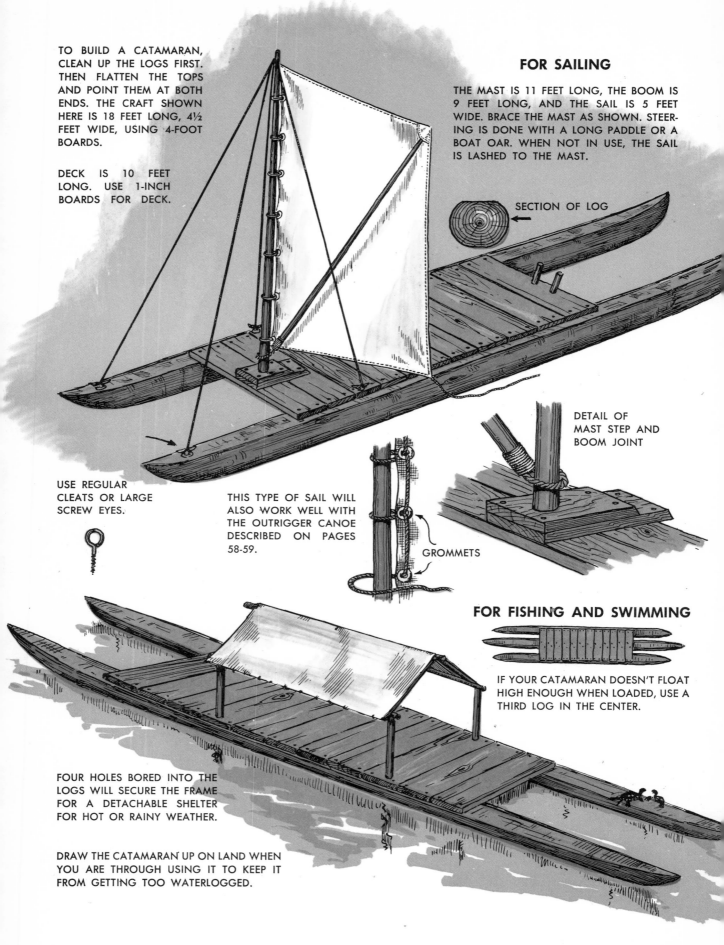

TO BUILD A CATAMARAN, CLEAN UP THE LOGS FIRST. THEN FLATTEN THE TOPS AND POINT THEM AT BOTH ENDS. THE CRAFT SHOWN HERE IS 18 FEET LONG, 4½ FEET WIDE, USING 4-FOOT BOARDS.

DECK IS 10 FEET LONG. USE 1-INCH BOARDS FOR DECK.

FOR SAILING

THE MAST IS 11 FEET LONG, THE BOOM IS 9 FEET LONG, AND THE SAIL IS 5 FEET WIDE. BRACE THE MAST AS SHOWN. STEERING IS DONE WITH A LONG PADDLE OR A BOAT OAR. WHEN NOT IN USE, THE SAIL IS LASHED TO THE MAST.

SECTION OF LOG

DETAIL OF MAST STEP AND BOOM JOINT

USE REGULAR CLEATS OR LARGE SCREW EYES.

THIS TYPE OF SAIL WILL ALSO WORK WELL WITH THE OUTRIGGER CANOE DESCRIBED ON PAGES 58-59.

GROMMETS

FOR FISHING AND SWIMMING

IF YOUR CATAMARAN DOESN'T FLOAT HIGH ENOUGH WHEN LOADED, USE A THIRD LOG IN THE CENTER.

FOUR HOLES BORED INTO THE LOGS WILL SECURE THE FRAME FOR A DETACHABLE SHELTER FOR HOT OR RAINY WEATHER.

DRAW THE CATAMARAN UP ON LAND WHEN YOU ARE THROUGH USING IT TO KEEP IT FROM GETTING TOO WATERLOGGED.

Building a Catamaran

WITH AN OUTBOARD MOTOR

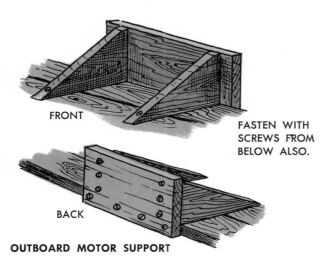

FRONT

FASTEN WITH SCREWS FROM BELOW ALSO.

BACK

OUTBOARD MOTOR SUPPORT

BE SURE YOUR MOTOR SUPPORT IS RIGID. USE SCREWS INSTEAD OF NAILS TO FASTEN IT TO THE PLATFORM.

The Fiji Islanders made a catamaran war canoe using three logs on which they fastened a platform and sail. Usually, catamarans are made from two logs fastened together by a wooden platform on which the natives kneel to paddle.

A catamaran is easy and inexpensive to build. You can have a lot of fun sailing it, since it is very sea-worthy.

You will need two dead logs, between 16 and 20 feet long and about 12 inches or more thick at the butt ends. Try them out for buoyancy first by floating them in the water, to be sure they are not waterlogged. For the platform planking, be sure to use 1-inch planks; lighter stock would sag too much.

PERHAPS IT'S A LONG SPAN BETWEEN A PRIMITIVE CATAMARAN AND AN OUTBOARD MOTOR, BUT THEY CERTAINLY MAKE A GOOD COMBINATION IN THE WATER.

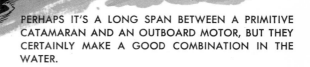

8" TO 10"

PUSH POLE

4" TO 6"

PERHAPS YOU'LL WANT TO USE A PUSH POLE. MAKE ONE LIKE THE SEMINOLE INDIANS USE, THE LENGTH DEPENDING ON THE LENGTH OF THE SAPLINGS AVAILABLE. THE WOODEN TRIANGLE KEEPS IT FROM SINKING INTO THE MUD.

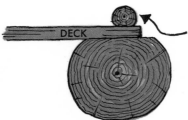

DECK

SAPLINGS SPIKED TO THE OUTER EDGES OF THE DECK WILL PROVIDE GOOD GRIPS FOR CLIMBING ABOARD WHEN SWIMMING AND WILL ALSO PREVENT YOUR GEAR FROM SLIPPING OVERBOARD TOO EASILY.

NOTICE THAT THE DECK BOARDS DO NOT EXTEND OVER THE LOGS. THIS PREVENTS SKINNED KNUCKLES. OTHER THINGS YOU CAN DO TO MAKE FOR MORE COMFORT ARE: SMOOTH LOGS WITH A DRAWKNIFE, USE BOARDS THAT ARE SMOOTH, CHAMFER ALL SHARP EDGES, AND REMOVE LOOSE SPLINTERS.

English Punt

A punt is a dandy boat for duck hunting, fishing, or hauling wood or supplies to camp. It can be poled, skulled, or rowed like a regular rowboat. To skull, place your skulling oar in the hole on the stern. A back-and-forth side motion will propel the boat forward.

Some of the best woods for building small boats are white pine, white cedar, or cypress. The sides should be ¾-inch dressed boards, so if you are going to plane them down yourself, get the boards thick enough in the first place to allow for this.

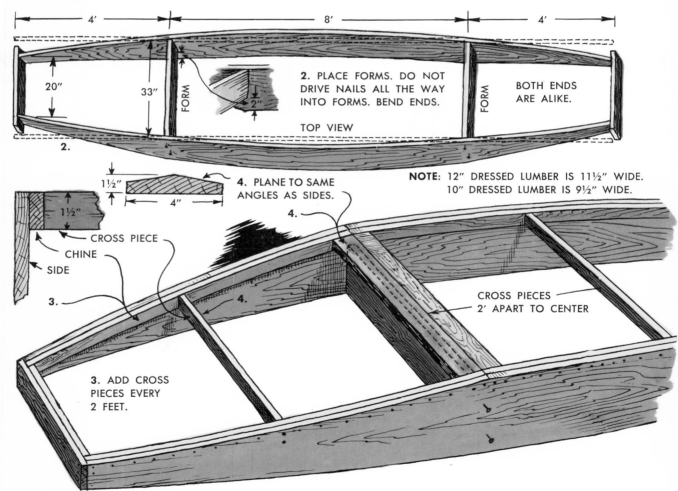

4'   8'   4'

20"   33"   FORM

2. PLACE FORMS. DO NOT DRIVE NAILS ALL THE WAY INTO FORMS. BEND ENDS.

2"

TOP VIEW

FORM   BOTH ENDS ARE ALIKE.

2.

1½"   4"   **4.** PLANE TO SAME ANGLES AS SIDES.

NOTE: 12" DRESSED LUMBER IS 11½" WIDE. 10" DRESSED LUMBER IS 9½" WIDE.

1½"

CROSS PIECE
CHINE
SIDE

3.   4.   4.

CROSS PIECES 2' APART TO CENTER

3. ADD CROSS PIECES EVERY 2 FEET.

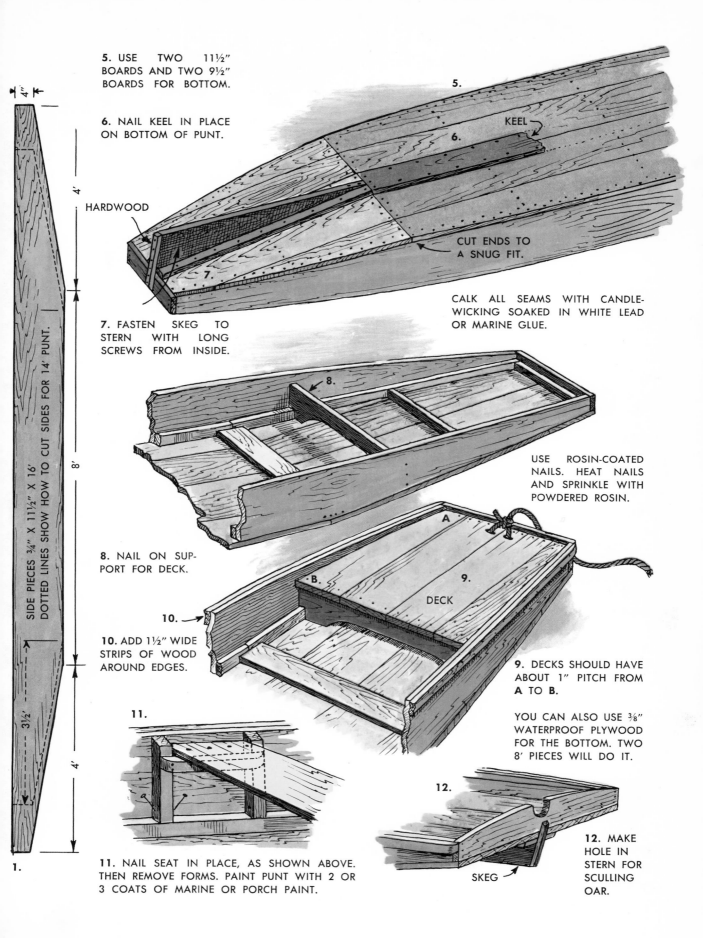

5. USE TWO 11½" BOARDS AND TWO 9½" BOARDS FOR BOTTOM.

6. NAIL KEEL IN PLACE ON BOTTOM OF PUNT.

HARDWOOD

KEEL

CUT ENDS TO A SNUG FIT.

CALK ALL SEAMS WITH CANDLE-WICKING SOAKED IN WHITE LEAD OR MARINE GLUE.

7. FASTEN SKEG TO STERN WITH LONG SCREWS FROM INSIDE.

USE ROSIN-COATED NAILS. HEAT NAILS AND SPRINKLE WITH POWDERED ROSIN.

8. NAIL ON SUP-PORT FOR DECK.

A

B.

DECK

10. ADD 1½" WIDE STRIPS OF WOOD AROUND EDGES.

9. DECKS SHOULD HAVE ABOUT 1" PITCH FROM **A** TO **B.**

YOU CAN ALSO USE ⅜" WATERPROOF PLYWOOD FOR THE BOTTOM. TWO 8' PIECES WILL DO IT.

SIDE PIECES ¾" X 11½" X 16'. DOTTED LINES SHOW HOW TO CUT SIDES FOR 14' PUNT.

4"

4'

8'

3½'

4'

1.

11.

11. NAIL SEAT IN PLACE, AS SHOWN ABOVE. THEN REMOVE FORMS. PAINT PUNT WITH 2 OR 3 COATS OF MARINE OR PORCH PAINT.

12.

SKEG

12. MAKE HOLE IN STERN FOR SCULLING OAR.

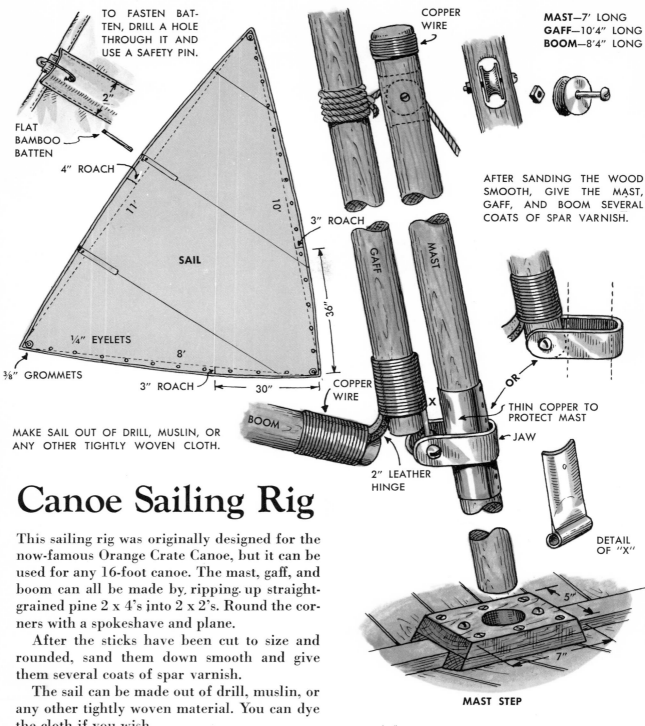

TO FASTEN BAT-
TEN, DRILL A HOLE
THROUGH IT AND
USE A SAFETY PIN.

2"

FLAT
BAMBOO
BATTEN

4" ROACH

11'

10'

SAIL

3" ROACH

1/4" EYELETS

8'

36"

3/8" GROMMETS

3" ROACH

30"

COPPER
WIRE

BOOM

MAKE SAIL OUT OF DRILL, MUSLIN, OR
ANY OTHER TIGHTLY WOVEN CLOTH.

COPPER
WIRE

MAST—7' LONG
GAFF—10'4" LONG
BOOM—8'4" LONG

AFTER SANDING THE WOOD
SMOOTH, GIVE THE MAST,
GAFF, AND BOOM SEVERAL
COATS OF SPAR VARNISH.

GAFF

MAST

X

OR

THIN COPPER TO
PROTECT MAST

JAW

2" LEATHER
HINGE

DETAIL
OF "X"

5"

7"

MAST STEP

OAK

MAST THWART
APPROX. 20"

FASTEN UNDER INWHALES
WITH FOUR R.H. SCREWS.

Canoe Sailing Rig

This sailing rig was originally designed for the now-famous Orange Crate Canoe, but it can be used for any 16-foot canoe. The mast, gaff, and boom can all be made by ripping up straight-grained pine 2 x 4's into 2 x 2's. Round the corners with a spokeshave and plane.

After the sticks have been cut to size and rounded, sand them down smooth and give them several coats of spar varnish.

The sail can be made out of drill, muslin, or any other tightly woven material. You can dye the cloth if you wish.

All of the edges should be hemmed with a good strong thread to prevent the sail from raveling or stretching out of shape. In each corner put a 3/8-inch grommet; in between the grommets on the 10-inch and 8-inch lengths, put 1/4-inch eyelets, approximately 8 to 10 inches apart.

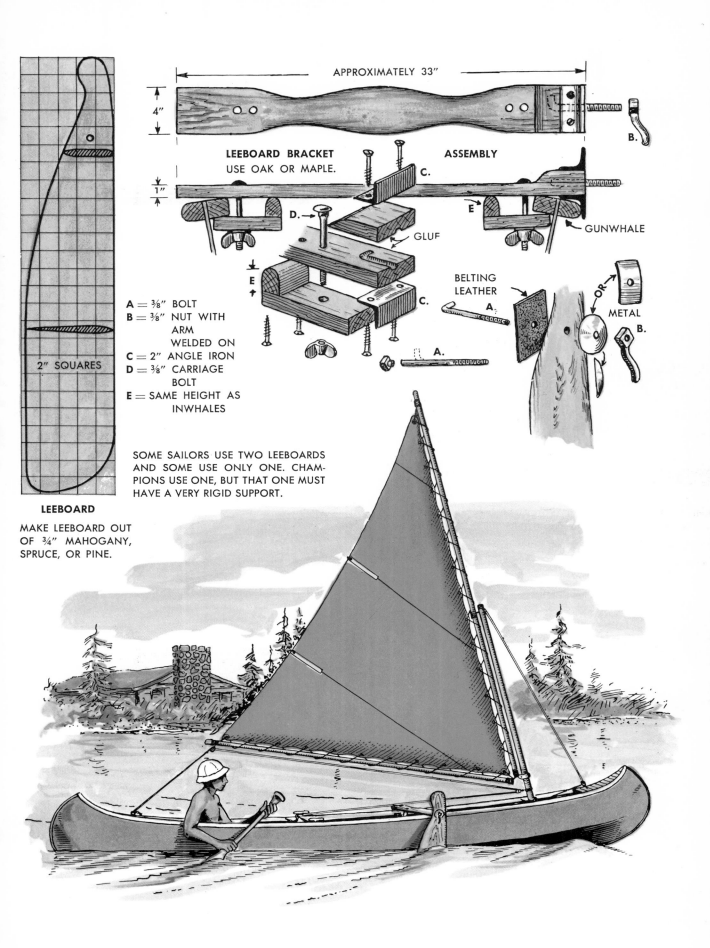

APPROXIMATELY 33"

4"

LEEBOARD BRACKET
USE OAK OR MAPLE.

ASSEMBLY

1"

C.

D.→

GLUE

E

GUNWHALE

E

BELTING
LEATHER

A.

OR

METAL

B.

2" SQUARES

A = ⅜" BOLT
B = ⅜" NUT WITH
ARM
WELDED ON
C = 2" ANGLE IRON
D = ⅜" CARRIAGE
BOLT
E = SAME HEIGHT AS
INWHALES

A.

SOME SAILORS USE TWO LEEBOARDS
AND SOME USE ONLY ONE. CHAM-
PIONS USE ONE, BUT THAT ONE MUST
HAVE A VERY RIGID SUPPORT.

LEEBOARD

MAKE LEEBOARD OUT
OF ¾" MAHOGANY,
SPRUCE, OR PINE.

IN ORDER TO MAKE RACING OFFICIAL, ALL BOATS SHOULD BE MADE ACCORDING TO THE SAME SPECIFICATIONS.

DON'T PUT BOAT IN THE WATER UNTIL IT HAS BEEN GIVEN ONE COAT OF PAINT AT LEAST.

BEFORE YOU START, GET TOGETHER ALL THE MATERIALS:
★ 7/8" OR 3/4" PINE CRATE LUMBER.
★ AN OLD PLASTIC TABLECLOTH, EITHER PLAIN OR FIGURED, FOR SAIL.
★ COLORED ENAMEL PAINTS.
★ AN ALUMINUM COOKIE SHEET, THIN COPPER OR BRASS, OR SOME TIN FOR THE KEEL AND RUDDER.
★ 1/2" ADHESIVE TAPE OR MASKING TAPE, TO BIND SAILS.
★ SPAR VARNISH FOR DECK, BOOM, AND MAST.
★ 3/8" BRASS OR IRON ROD, OR OTHER METAL, TO WEIGHT KEEL.

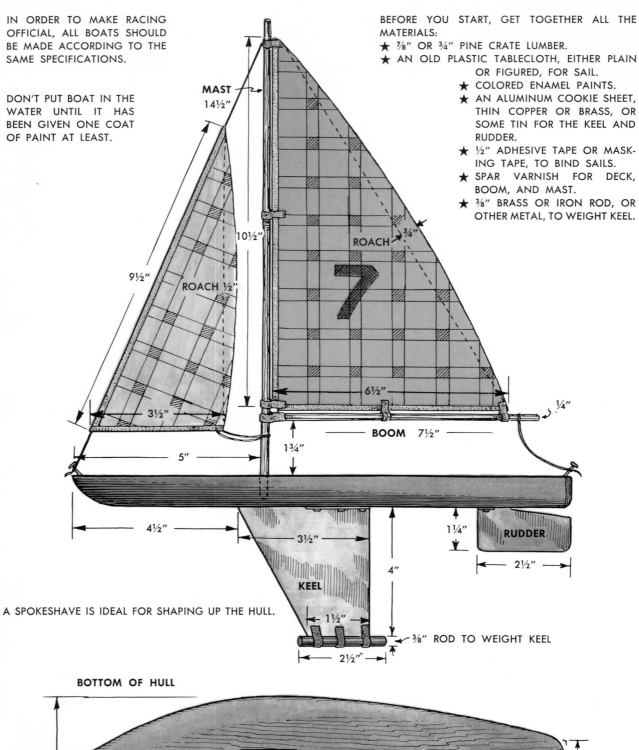

A SPOKESHAVE IS IDEAL FOR SHAPING UP THE HULL.

60

Model Racing Sloops

If you live or camp near a lake or pond, you and your friends can have a lot of good sport racing these trim little model sloops.

If the race is to be absolutely fair, all boats should be made from the same specifications. Assign a number to each of the sloops in the race so that they can be identified easily while under sail.

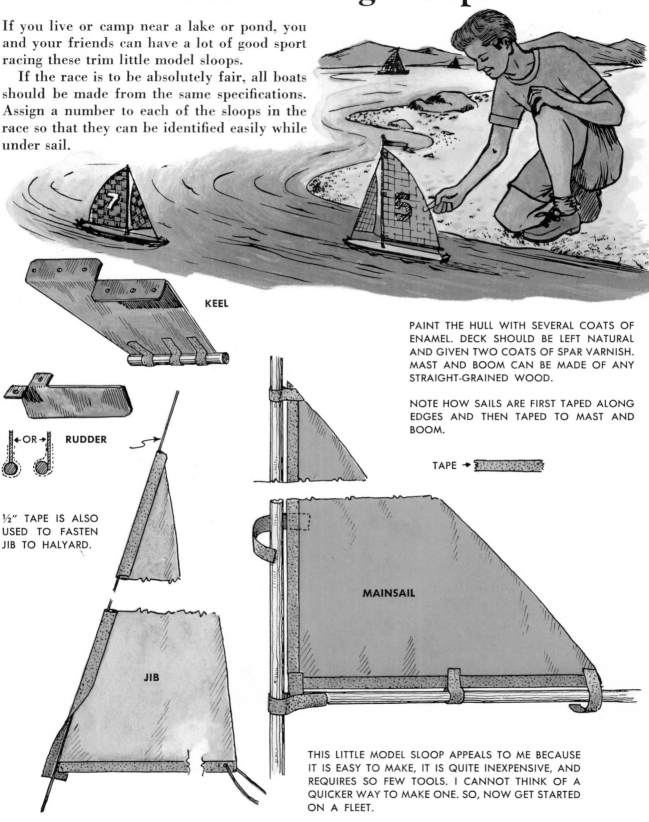

KEEL

RUDDER

←OR→

½" TAPE IS ALSO USED TO FASTEN JIB TO HALYARD.

JIB

MAINSAIL

PAINT THE HULL WITH SEVERAL COATS OF ENAMEL. DECK SHOULD BE LEFT NATURAL AND GIVEN TWO COATS OF SPAR VARNISH. MAST AND BOOM CAN BE MADE OF ANY STRAIGHT-GRAINED WOOD.

NOTE HOW SAILS ARE FIRST TAPED ALONG EDGES AND THEN TAPED TO MAST AND BOOM.

TAPE →

THIS LITTLE MODEL SLOOP APPEALS TO ME BECAUSE IT IS EASY TO MAKE, IT IS QUITE INEXPENSIVE, AND REQUIRES SO FEW TOOLS. I CANNOT THINK OF A QUICKER WAY TO MAKE ONE. SO, NOW GET STARTED ON A FLEET.

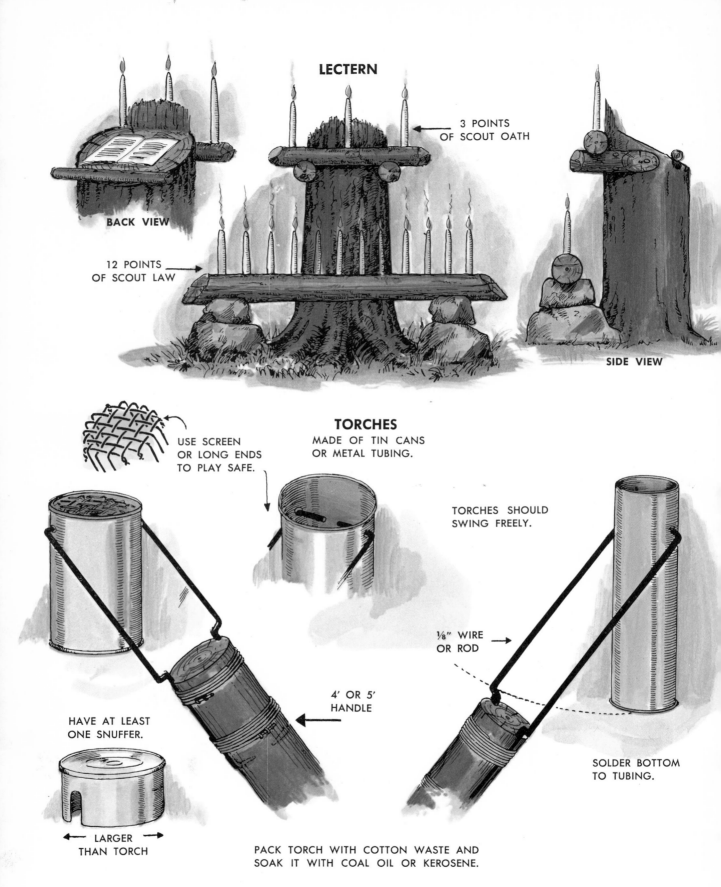

LECTERN

BACK VIEW

3 POINTS
OF SCOUT OATH

12 POINTS
OF SCOUT LAW

SIDE VIEW

USE SCREEN
OR LONG ENDS
TO PLAY SAFE.

TORCHES
MADE OF TIN CANS
OR METAL TUBING.

TORCHES SHOULD
SWING FREELY.

$\frac{1}{8}$" WIRE
OR ROD

4' OR 5'
HANDLE

HAVE AT LEAST
ONE SNUFFER.

SOLDER BOTTOM
TO TUBING.

← LARGER →
THAN TORCH

PACK TORCH WITH COTTON WASTE AND
SOAK IT WITH COAL OIL OR KEROSENE.

Ceremonial Aids

Of all the wonderful experiences you will have at camp, the camp-fire programs will probably remain in your memory the longest. You will particularly remember how well the leaders conducted the entire program. But what you didn't know was that some of the fans and rattles used in the ceremonies had the lines that the leaders were to say printed on the back of them. Here are some ideas for next year's program.

MEMORY AIDS

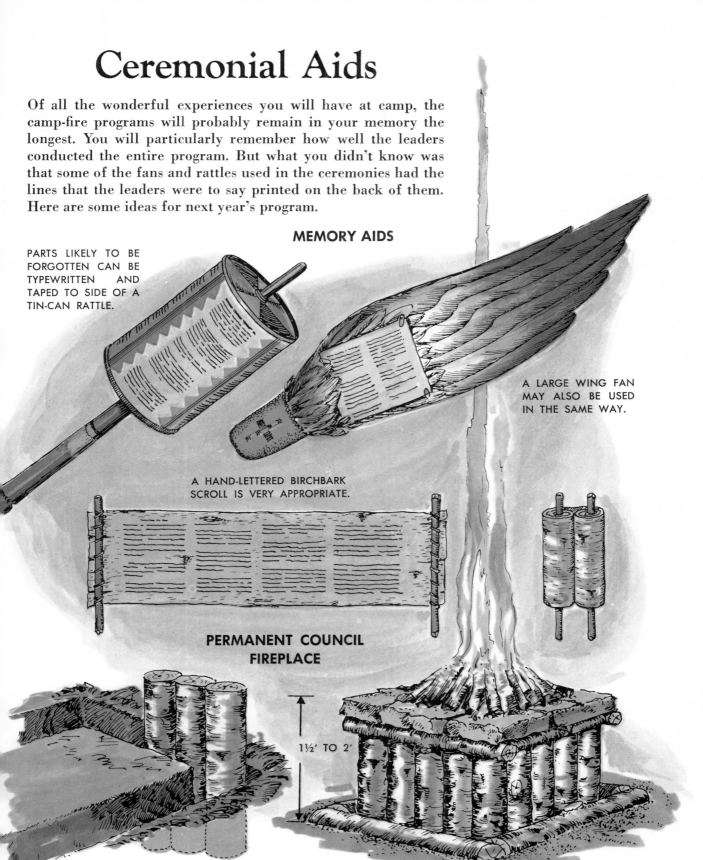

PARTS LIKELY TO BE FORGOTTEN CAN BE TYPEWRITTEN AND TAPED TO SIDE OF A TIN-CAN RATTLE.

A LARGE WING FAN MAY ALSO BE USED IN THE SAME WAY.

A HAND-LETTERED BIRCHBARK SCROLL IS VERY APPROPRIATE.

PERMANENT COUNCIL FIREPLACE

1½' TO 2'

DIG TRENCH ABOUT 3 FEET SQUARE. FILL WITH EARTH AND COVER WITH FLAT STONES.

Camp-fire Awards

Here are some good ideas for camp-fire awards that can be made out of materials found right in the camp area. These will be never-to-be-forgotten mementos for anyone who receives one.

The lettering on these awards can be painted, carved, or burned in with a hot iron. It is always a good idea to provide space on the back of the award where everyone in the ceremony can sign it. Always be sure to include the date so that in future years there is no argument as to when it was made.

Just remember, at a camp-fire presentation nothing looks quite so inadequate as a "store-bought" award. So go to it and make some striking ones for your ceremonies.

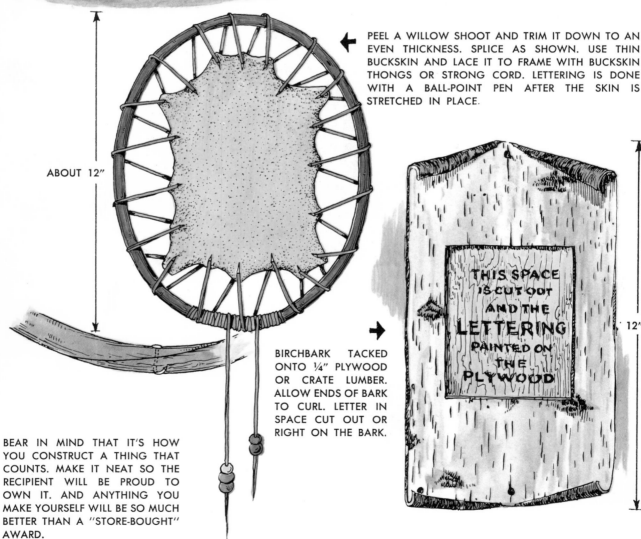

ABOUT 12"

PEEL A WILLOW SHOOT AND TRIM IT DOWN TO AN EVEN THICKNESS. SPLICE AS SHOWN. USE THIN BUCKSKIN AND LACE IT TO FRAME WITH BUCKSKIN THONGS OR STRONG CORD. LETTERING IS DONE WITH A BALL-POINT PEN AFTER THE SKIN IS STRETCHED IN PLACE.

BIRCHBARK TACKED ONTO ¼" PLYWOOD OR CRATE LUMBER. ALLOW ENDS OF BARK TO CURL. LETTER IN SPACE CUT OUT OR RIGHT ON THE BARK.

THIS SPACE IS CUT OUT AND THE LETTERING PAINTED ON THE PLYWOOD

12"

BEAR IN MIND THAT IT'S HOW YOU CONSTRUCT A THING THAT COUNTS. MAKE IT NEAT SO THE RECIPIENT WILL BE PROUD TO OWN IT. AND ANYTHING YOU MAKE YOURSELF WILL BE SO MUCH BETTER THAN A "STORE-BOUGHT" AWARD.

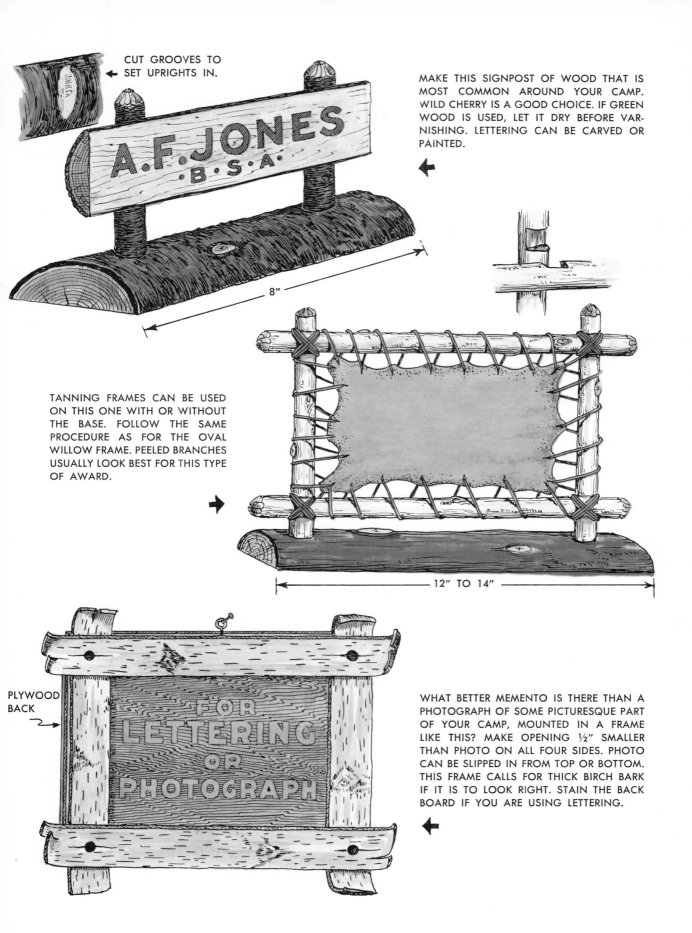

CUT GROOVES TO SET UPRIGHTS IN.

A.F. JONES
·B·S·A·

8"

MAKE THIS SIGNPOST OF WOOD THAT IS MOST COMMON AROUND YOUR CAMP. WILD CHERRY IS A GOOD CHOICE. IF GREEN WOOD IS USED, LET IT DRY BEFORE VARNISHING. LETTERING CAN BE CARVED OR PAINTED.

TANNING FRAMES CAN BE USED ON THIS ONE WITH OR WITHOUT THE BASE. FOLLOW THE SAME PROCEDURE AS FOR THE OVAL WILLOW FRAME. PEELED BRANCHES USUALLY LOOK BEST FOR THIS TYPE OF AWARD.

12" TO 14"

PLYWOOD BACK

FOR LETTERING OR PHOTOGRAPH

WHAT BETTER MEMENTO IS THERE THAN A PHOTOGRAPH OF SOME PICTURESQUE PART OF YOUR CAMP, MOUNTED IN A FRAME LIKE THIS? MAKE OPENING ½" SMALLER THAN PHOTO ON ALL FOUR SIDES. PHOTO CAN BE SLIPPED IN FROM TOP OR BOTTOM. THIS FRAME CALLS FOR THICK BIRCH BARK IF IT IS TO LOOK RIGHT. STAIN THE BACK BOARD IF YOU ARE USING LETTERING.

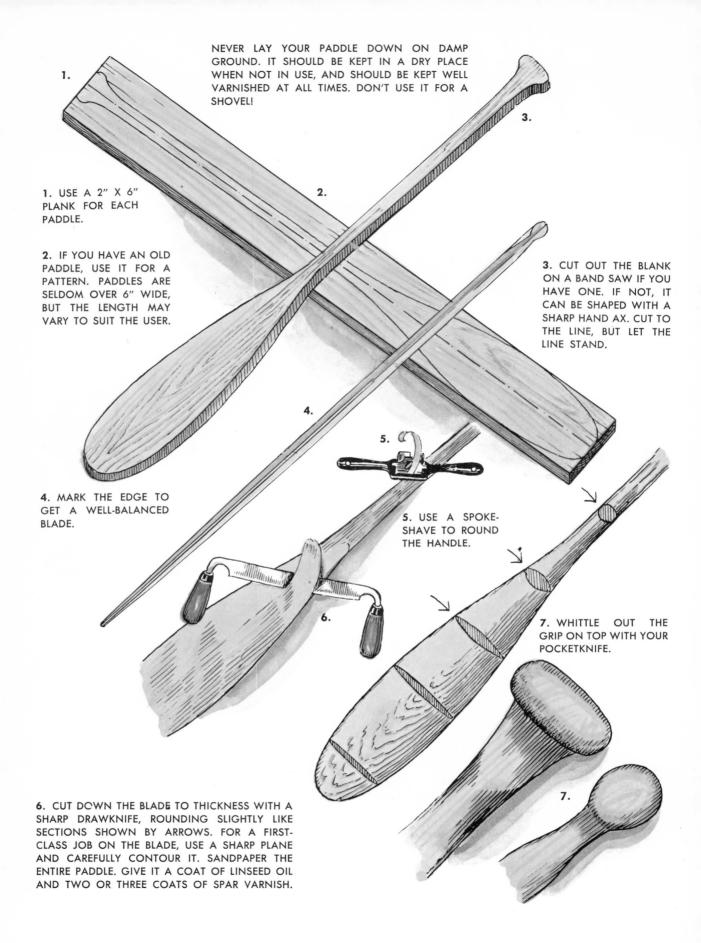

NEVER LAY YOUR PADDLE DOWN ON DAMP GROUND. IT SHOULD BE KEPT IN A DRY PLACE WHEN NOT IN USE, AND SHOULD BE KEPT WELL VARNISHED AT ALL TIMES. DON'T USE IT FOR A SHOVEL!

1. USE A 2" X 6" PLANK FOR EACH PADDLE.

2. IF YOU HAVE AN OLD PADDLE, USE IT FOR A PATTERN. PADDLES ARE SELDOM OVER 6" WIDE, BUT THE LENGTH MAY VARY TO SUIT THE USER.

3. CUT OUT THE BLANK ON A BAND SAW IF YOU HAVE ONE. IF NOT, IT CAN BE SHAPED WITH A SHARP HAND AX. CUT TO THE LINE, BUT LET THE LINE STAND.

4. MARK THE EDGE TO GET A WELL-BALANCED BLADE.

5. USE A SPOKE-SHAVE TO ROUND THE HANDLE.

6. CUT DOWN THE BLADE TO THICKNESS WITH A SHARP DRAWKNIFE, ROUNDING SLIGHTLY LIKE SECTIONS SHOWN BY ARROWS. FOR A FIRST-CLASS JOB ON THE BLADE, USE A SHARP PLANE AND CAREFULLY CONTOUR IT. SANDPAPER THE ENTIRE PADDLE. GIVE IT A COAT OF LINSEED OIL AND TWO OR THREE COATS OF SPAR VARNISH.

7. WHITTLE OUT THE GRIP ON TOP WITH YOUR POCKETKNIFE.

Making Canoe Paddles

Canoe paddles are not difficult to make. Use straight-grained spruce or white cedar, 1¼ inches thick, 6 to 10 inches wide, and 6 feet long. These two woods are very easy to work with, and most of the work can be done with a good sharp drawknife.

Decorate your paddle with any design you choose that fits the shape of the paddle. If your paddle is a memento of camp or some other experience, you will want to include the name of the camp, the year, and some of your buddies' signatures on the paddle.

THIS IS A STEERING PADDLE. IT IS POINTED TO STICK INTO THE GROUND TO ANCHOR THE CANOE.

TO DECORATE PADDLES, USE COLORED ENAMELS AND FINISH WITH TWO COATS OF SPAR VARNISH.

NOTE: LEAVE THE WOOD NATURAL FOR THE BACKGROUNDS. THAT IS, DON'T PAINT ENTIRE PADDLE.

REGION 7 CANOE BASE

NORTHWEST COAST

MODERN DESIGNS

SOUTH SEA ISLANDS

1. CUT OUT OPENING WITH CAN OPENER OR A SMALL PAIR OF TIN SNIPS. STRAIGHTEN OUT EDGES AND FILE OFF ANY SHARP POINTS OF TIN.

1.

2⅝″

1¼″

2.

2. CUT OFF TOP OF TIN CAN AND PUNCH HOLE IN CENTER OF BOTTOM FOR BOLT. DO THE SAME WITH BOTTOM OF TIN CAN.

5½″   ¾″   2⅝″

2⅞″

1¼″

PUNCH HOLES FOR ¼″ STOVE BOLTS.

3.

3. PUNCH VENTS IN ENDS AND HOLES FOR BOLTS IN BOTTOM OF CAN.

4.

4. BOLT CANS TO BOTTOM.

Camp Stove

My good friend, Carl Beninghaus, left me one of these little stoves one day, and I have found it to be one of the handiest gadgets that I have ever taken along on a hike. It is light weight and takes up very little space in a pack. You never have to worry about having to find dry wood in a rain, and your fire is always just right for cooking.

All you need to make one of these stoves is a one-quart flat tin can, tin snips, one small round tin can, a small punch, a few small bolts, and some galvanized wire screening.

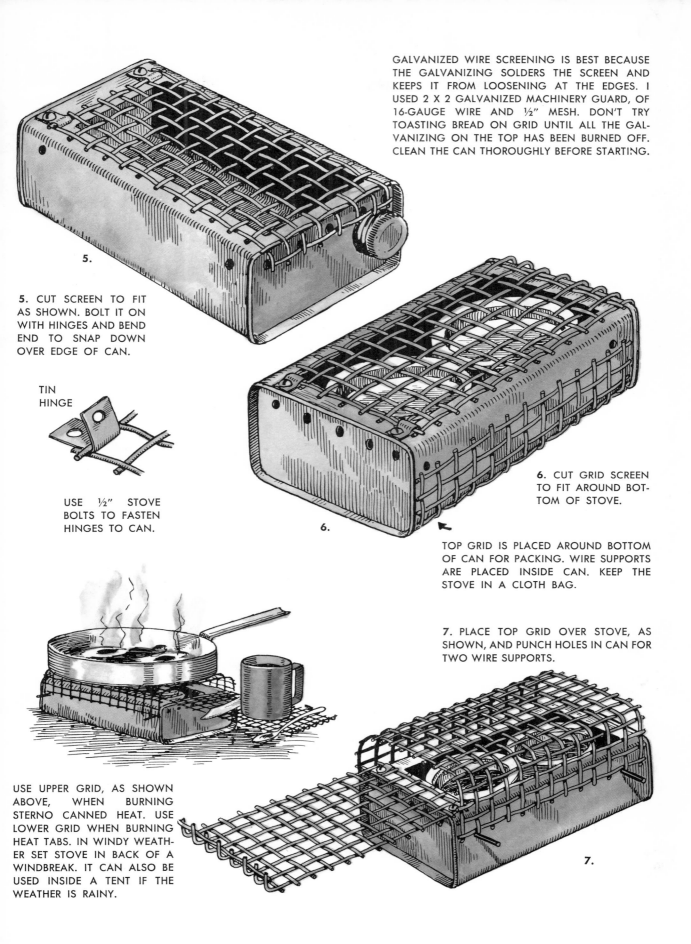

GALVANIZED WIRE SCREENING IS BEST BECAUSE THE GALVANIZING SOLDERS THE SCREEN AND KEEPS IT FROM LOOSENING AT THE EDGES. I USED 2 X 2 GALVANIZED MACHINERY GUARD, OF 16-GAUGE WIRE AND ½" MESH. DON'T TRY TOASTING BREAD ON GRID UNTIL ALL THE GALVANIZING ON THE TOP HAS BEEN BURNED OFF. CLEAN THE CAN THOROUGHLY BEFORE STARTING.

5.

5. CUT SCREEN TO FIT AS SHOWN. BOLT IT ON WITH HINGES AND BEND END TO SNAP DOWN OVER EDGE OF CAN.

TIN HINGE

USE ½" STOVE BOLTS TO FASTEN HINGES TO CAN.

6.

6. CUT GRID SCREEN TO FIT AROUND BOTTOM OF STOVE.

TOP GRID IS PLACED AROUND BOTTOM OF CAN FOR PACKING. WIRE SUPPORTS ARE PLACED INSIDE CAN. KEEP THE STOVE IN A CLOTH BAG.

7. PLACE TOP GRID OVER STOVE, AS SHOWN, AND PUNCH HOLES IN CAN FOR TWO WIRE SUPPORTS.

USE UPPER GRID, AS SHOWN ABOVE, WHEN BURNING STERNO CANNED HEAT. USE LOWER GRID WHEN BURNING HEAT TABS. IN WINDY WEATHER SET STOVE IN BACK OF A WINDBREAK. IT CAN ALSO BE USED INSIDE A TENT IF THE WEATHER IS RAINY.

7.

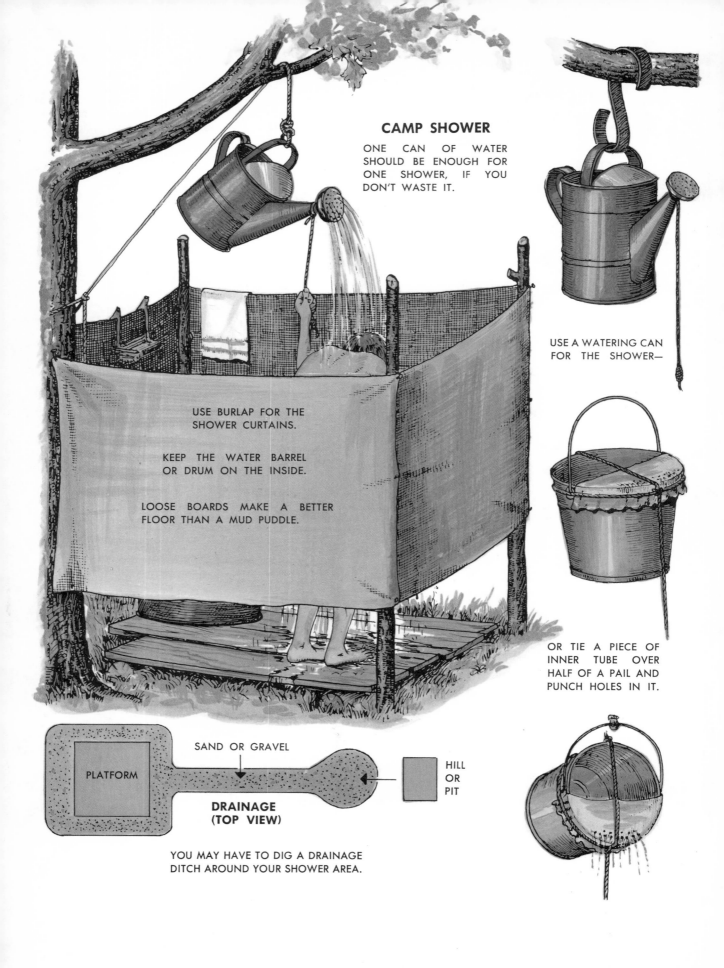

CAMP SHOWER

ONE CAN OF WATER SHOULD BE ENOUGH FOR ONE SHOWER, IF YOU DON'T WASTE IT.

USE BURLAP FOR THE SHOWER CURTAINS.

KEEP THE WATER BARREL OR DRUM ON THE INSIDE.

LOOSE BOARDS MAKE A BETTER FLOOR THAN A MUD PUDDLE.

USE A WATERING CAN FOR THE SHOWER—

OR TIE A PIECE OF INNER TUBE OVER HALF OF A PAIL AND PUNCH HOLES IN IT.

PLATFORM

SAND OR GRAVEL

HILL OR PIT

DRAINAGE (TOP VIEW)

YOU MAY HAVE TO DIG A DRAINAGE DITCH AROUND YOUR SHOWER AREA.

Camp Shower and Wash Fountain

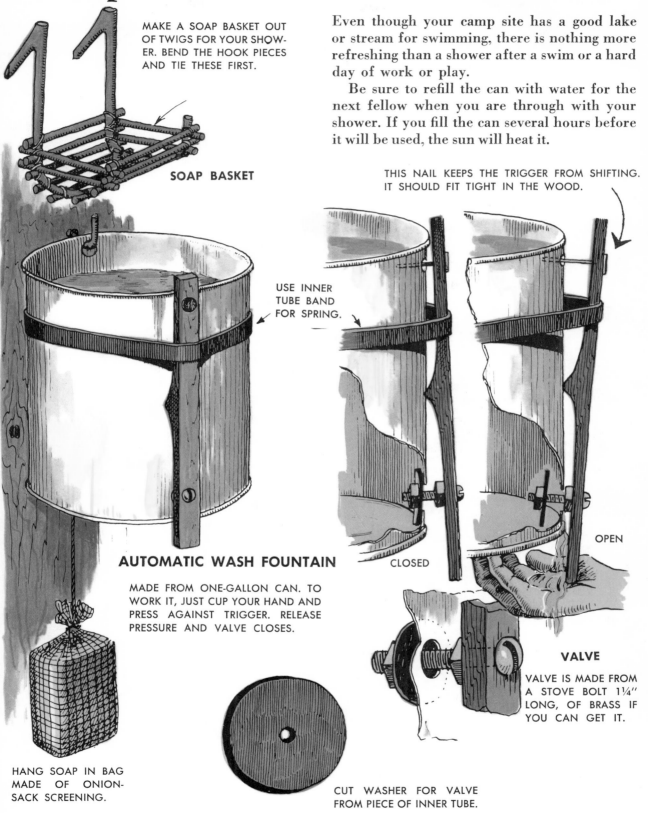

MAKE A SOAP BASKET OUT OF TWIGS FOR YOUR SHOWER. BEND THE HOOK PIECES AND TIE THESE FIRST.

Even though your camp site has a good lake or stream for swimming, there is nothing more refreshing than a shower after a swim or a hard day of work or play.

Be sure to refill the can with water for the next fellow when you are through with your shower. If you fill the can several hours before it will be used, the sun will heat it.

SOAP BASKET

THIS NAIL KEEPS THE TRIGGER FROM SHIFTING. IT SHOULD FIT TIGHT IN THE WOOD.

USE INNER TUBE BAND FOR SPRING.

AUTOMATIC WASH FOUNTAIN

MADE FROM ONE-GALLON CAN. TO WORK IT, JUST CUP YOUR HAND AND PRESS AGAINST TRIGGER. RELEASE PRESSURE AND VALVE CLOSES.

CLOSED

OPEN

HANG SOAP IN BAG MADE OF ONION-SACK SCREENING.

CUT WASHER FOR VALVE FROM PIECE OF INNER TUBE.

VALVE

VALVE IS MADE FROM A STOVE BOLT 1¼" LONG, OF BRASS IF YOU CAN GET IT.

Going Fishing

One of the first things a good fisherman should know is how to tie easily and quickly the knots that are used to attach the lines which hold leaders, plugs, and hooks. There is nothing more disappointing than to lose that "big one" because of a badly tied line. Practice these knots in your spare time, and the next time the gang wants to go fishing, you will be all set. It is easier to tie these knots than it looks in the pictures.

SIMPLE END LOOP OR LARK'S HEAD

THIS KNOT IS AN EASY ONE, GOOD FOR TYING LINE TO LEADER, OR LEADER TO HOOK OR PLUG.

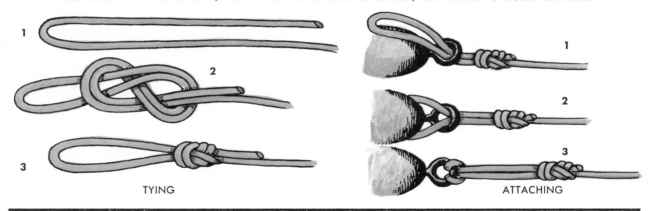

TYING

ATTACHING

PERFECTION LOOP

HERE'S A KNOT FOR THE END OF YOUR LEADER THAT YOU CAN COUNT ON.

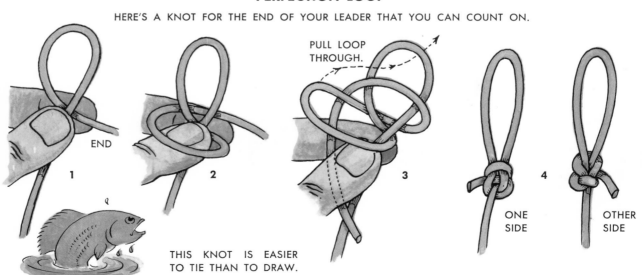

PULL LOOP THROUGH.

END

THIS KNOT IS EASIER TO TIE THAN TO DRAW.

ONE SIDE

OTHER SIDE

TYING NYLON OR GUT LEADERS

YOU'LL LIKE DOING THIS KNOT ONCE YOU GET THE FEEL OF IT.

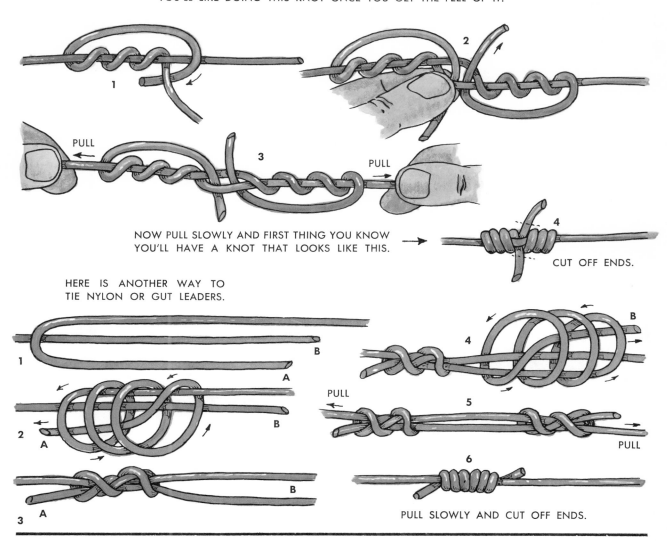

NOW PULL SLOWLY AND FIRST THING YOU KNOW YOU'LL HAVE A KNOT THAT LOOKS LIKE THIS.

CUT OFF ENDS.

HERE IS ANOTHER WAY TO TIE NYLON OR GUT LEADERS.

PULL SLOWLY AND CUT OFF ENDS.

DROP LOOP

THIS IS A GOOD KNOT FOR ATTACHING AN EXTRA GUTTED HOOK TO YOUR LEADER. IT'S FUN TO TIE. TRY IT AND SEE HOW NICELY IT WORKS.

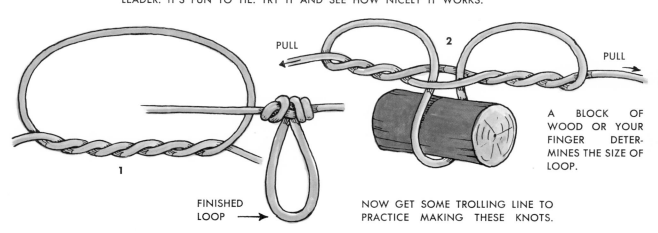

FINISHED LOOP →

A BLOCK OF WOOD OR YOUR FINGER DETERMINES THE SIZE OF LOOP.

NOW GET SOME TROLLING LINE TO PRACTICE MAKING THESE KNOTS.

Corkers and Bass Bugs

Make up a few of these corkers and you will be surprised at the action you will get the next time you go fishing for bluegills, crappies, and bass.

MATERIALS

USE SILK THREAD IF YOU HAVE IT. IF YOU DO NOT HAVE BUCKTAIL, USE ANOTHER KIND OF WHITE HAIR OR SOME WHITE FEATHERS.

THIS IS A DINGER

1.

SLOT FOR HOOK

1. THIS IS HOW TO SHAPE THE CORK. NOTCHES ON THE SIDES ARE FOR BUNCHES OF HAIR. USE A SHARP KNIFE AND SANDPAPER.

2.

2. PUT CEMENT IN SLOT. PUSH HOOK DOWN AND PUT MORE CEMENT IN SLOT.

⅛″

3.

3. PINCH SLOT SHUT BY SQUEEZING AND WRAPPING IT WITH HEAVY THREAD FROM FRONT TO BACK, ABOUT ⅛″ APART. PAINT OVER THREAD WITH TWO COATS OF WHITE DOPE. LET IT DRY.

4.

4. PREPARE TWO BUNCHES OF WHITE BUCKTAIL HAIR BY TYING THEM WITH THREAD. DIP ENDS IN CEMENT.

5.

5. TIE BUNCHES IN THE NOTCHES TO MAKE A COLLAR AND WIND IN CEMENT. CLIP OFF ENDS OF HAIR IN FRONT AND PAINT ENDS AND COLLAR WHITE.

IT SHOULD LOOK LIKE THIS WHEN IT'S FINISHED. TRY ONE WITH A RED COLLAR, TOO.

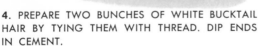

HERE'S A DEADLY BLACK WIDOW

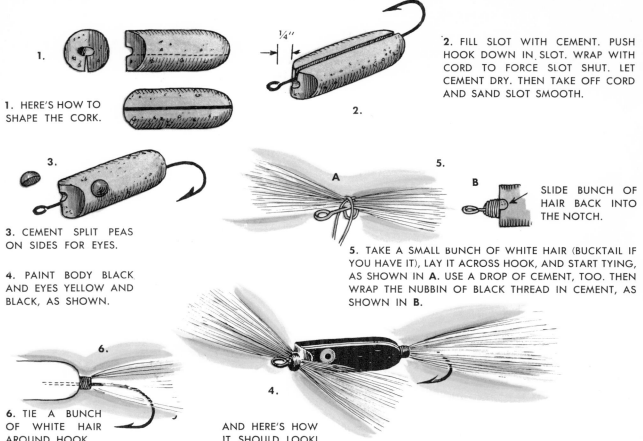

1. HERE'S HOW TO SHAPE THE CORK.

1/4"

2. FILL SLOT WITH CEMENT. PUSH HOOK DOWN IN SLOT. WRAP WITH CORD TO FORCE SLOT SHUT. LET CEMENT DRY. THEN TAKE OFF CORD AND SAND SLOT SMOOTH.

3. CEMENT SPLIT PEAS ON SIDES FOR EYES.

4. PAINT BODY BLACK AND EYES YELLOW AND BLACK, AS SHOWN.

A   B   SLIDE BUNCH OF HAIR BACK INTO THE NOTCH.

5. TAKE A SMALL BUNCH OF WHITE HAIR (BUCKTAIL IF YOU HAVE IT), LAY IT ACROSS HOOK, AND START TYING, AS SHOWN IN **A.** USE A DROP OF CEMENT, TOO. THEN WRAP THE NUBBIN OF BLACK THREAD IN CEMENT, AS SHOWN IN **B.**

6. TIE A BUNCH OF WHITE HAIR AROUND HOOK.

AND HERE'S HOW IT SHOULD LOOK!

A NEAT TRICK

WHEN THE FISH ARE LAZY AND STRIKE SHORT, TRY THIS LITTLE TRICK. IT REALLY WORKS!

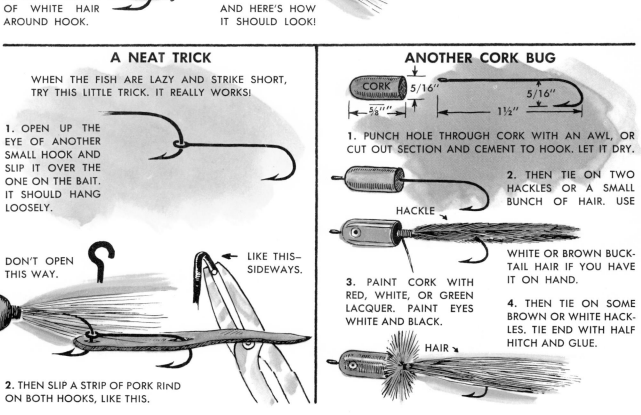

1. OPEN UP THE EYE OF ANOTHER SMALL HOOK AND SLIP IT OVER THE ONE ON THE BAIT. IT SHOULD HANG LOOSELY.

DON'T OPEN THIS WAY.

LIKE THIS— SIDEWAYS.

2. THEN SLIP A STRIP OF PORK RIND ON BOTH HOOKS, LIKE THIS.

ANOTHER CORK BUG

CORK   5/16"   5/16"
5/8"   1½"

1. PUNCH HOLE THROUGH CORK WITH AN AWL, OR CUT OUT SECTION AND CEMENT TO HOOK. LET IT DRY.

HACKLE

2. THEN TIE ON TWO HACKLES OR A SMALL BUNCH OF HAIR. USE

WHITE OR BROWN BUCK-TAIL HAIR IF YOU HAVE IT ON HAND.

3. PAINT CORK WITH RED, WHITE, OR GREEN LACQUER. PAINT EYES WHITE AND BLACK.

4. THEN TIE ON SOME BROWN OR WHITE HACK-LES. TIE END WITH HALF HITCH AND GLUE.

HAIR

Leather Letter Folder

A well-made letter folder will be appreciated by anyone who carries an assortment of cards, papers, and notes in his coat pocket. It makes a wonderful Father's Day present, or a good Christmas present for your older brother.

Use either a smooth- or rough-grained leather of good quality. If it is grained, select the most evenly matched pieces. The outer piece, or cover, should be about 1/16-inch thick, and the inner divider a bit thinner. Use laces of goat or calf skin. Skive the edges where two or more pieces are laced together to eliminate a bulky appearance.

You can emboss designs or initials on the outer flap to suit your fancy. Use the same method for embossing as used on the knife sheath, described on the following two pages.

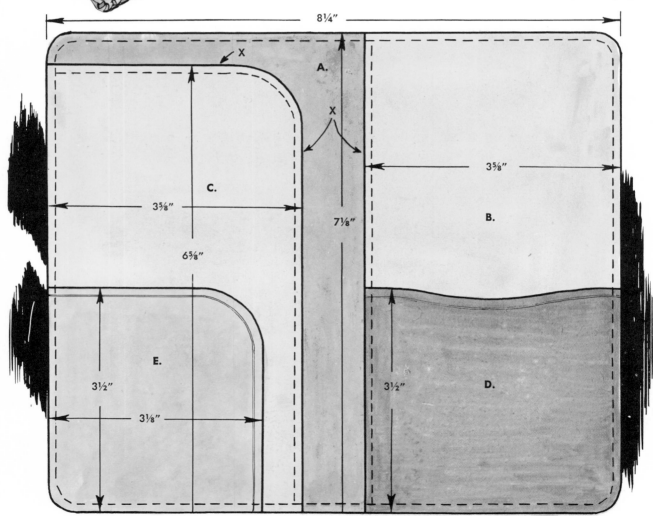

1. CUT OUT THE FIVE PIECES: **A, B, C, D,** AND **E.**

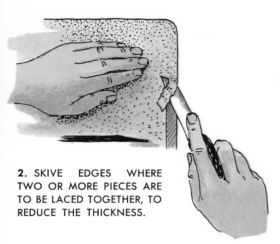

2. SKIVE EDGES WHERE TWO OR MORE PIECES ARE TO BE LACED TOGETHER, TO REDUCE THE THICKNESS.

3. PUNCH SLOTS ON EDGES **X** OF **C** AND **B** AND LACE WITH OVERCAST STITCH.

4. CEMENT EDGES TOGETHER TO KEEP THEM FROM SLIPPING WHILE YOU PUNCH REMAINING SLOTS.

5. LACE OUTER EDGES.

LACING

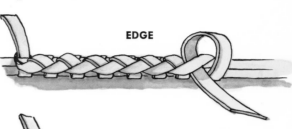

EDGE

FRONT

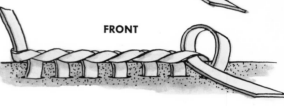

PUNCHING

USE A SINGLE- AND A THREE-PRONG CHISEL FOR PUNCHING SLOTS, AND A FID FOR ENLARGING THEM.

FID

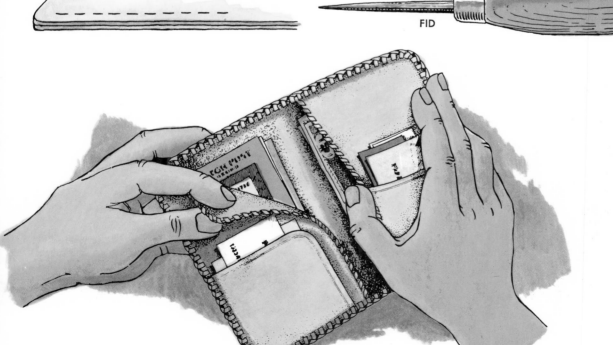

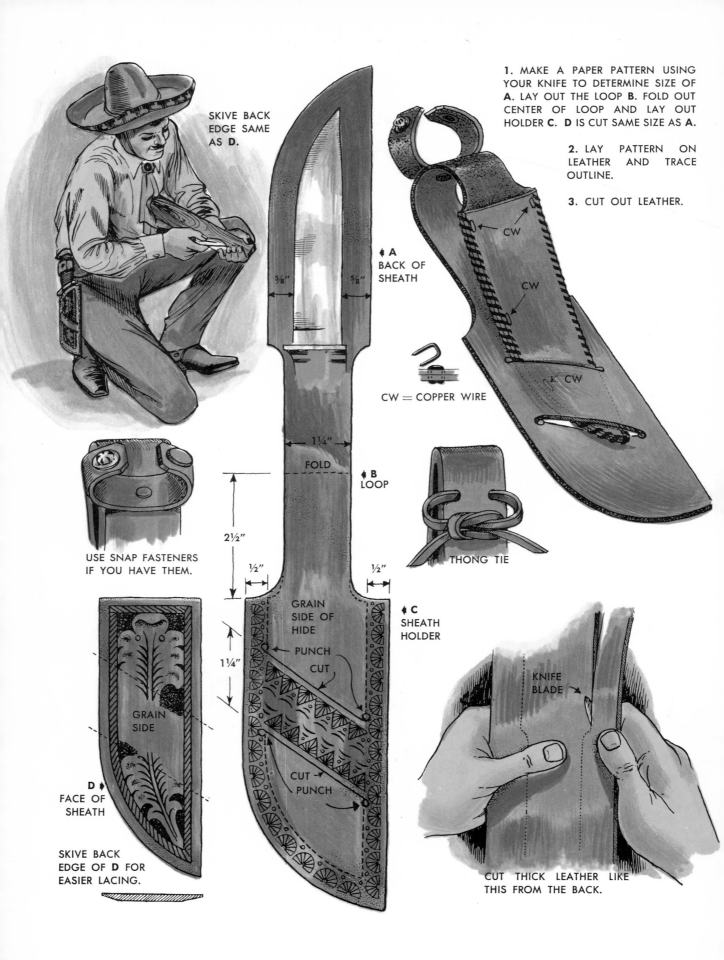

SKIVE BACK EDGE SAME AS **D.**

1. MAKE A PAPER PATTERN USING YOUR KNIFE TO DETERMINE SIZE OF **A.** LAY OUT THE LOOP **B.** FOLD OUT CENTER OF LOOP AND LAY OUT HOLDER **C. D** IS CUT SAME SIZE AS **A.**

2. LAY PATTERN ON LEATHER AND TRACE OUTLINE.

3. CUT OUT LEATHER.

5/8" 5/8"

A
BACK OF SHEATH

CW
CW
CW

CW = COPPER WIRE

USE SNAP FASTENERS IF YOU HAVE THEM.

1¼"

FOLD

B
LOOP

2½"

½" ½"

GRAIN SIDE OF HIDE

PUNCH CUT

C
SHEATH HOLDER

THONG TIE

1¼"

GRAIN SIDE

CUT PUNCH

KNIFE BLADE

D
FACE OF SHEATH

SKIVE BACK EDGE OF **D** FOR EASIER LACING.

CUT THICK LEATHER LIKE THIS FROM THE BACK.

Mexican Knife Sheath

No straight-blade knife should be worn, carried, or stored without being sheathed in a holder to protect the person carrying it and to keep the knife from becoming dull and rusty.

Sheaths can be made from wood, leather, or plastic. I made mine from a piece of old cowhide. The leather should be rather stiff. For the laces you can use leather shoe laces or cut thin leather to ⅛-inch wide. For lacing, see the instructions given under making a letter folder on page 77.

Make the stamping tools out of old 20-penny spikes, as shown. Practice your designs on a spare piece of leather until you can tell how hard you will need to hammer the stamping tool. Try out different designs and patterns with the tools you make by using them in combinations with each other.

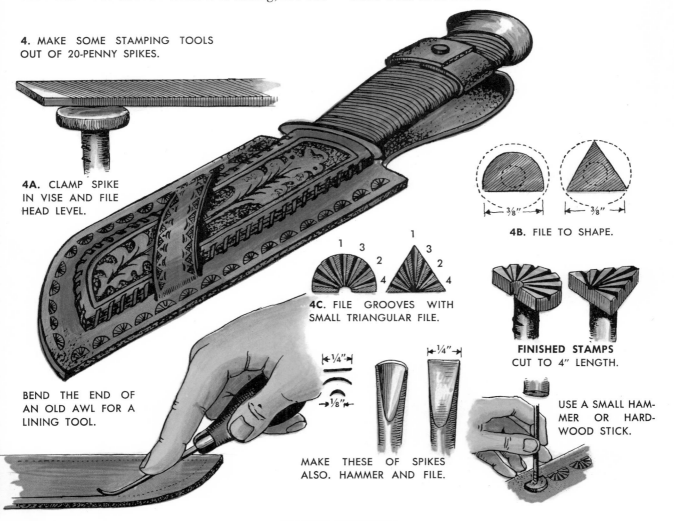

4. MAKE SOME STAMPING TOOLS OUT OF 20-PENNY SPIKES.

4A. CLAMP SPIKE IN VISE AND FILE HEAD LEVEL.

4B. FILE TO SHAPE.

4C. FILE GROOVES WITH SMALL TRIANGULAR FILE.

FINISHED STAMPS CUT TO 4" LENGTH.

BEND THE END OF AN OLD AWL FOR A LINING TOOL.

MAKE THESE OF SPIKES ALSO. HAMMER AND FILE.

USE A SMALL HAMMER OR HARDWOOD STICK.

TOOLING PROCEDURE

1. TRACE OR DRAW DESIGN ON **D** WITH BLUNT POINT OF AWL. **2.** MOISTEN LEATHER FROM THE BACK UNTIL MOISTURE SHOWS ON SURFACE. **3.** RUB OUTLINE OF ROPE BORDER WITH LINING TOOL AND PUNCH CROSS LINES WITH ¼" CHISEL STAMP. **4.** OUTLINE LEAF AND HAMMER DOWN BACKGROUND WITH SMALL NAIL SET. **5.** FINISH LEAF WITH LINER AND ¼" CURVED STAMP. **6.** PUNCH AND CUT SLOTS IN **C**. **7.** MOISTEN **C** AND STAMP AS SHOWN. **8.** AFTER LEATHER HAS DRIED OUT THOROUGHLY, PLACE **D** AND **A** TOGETHER, PUNCH SLOTS AND LACE AS SHOWN AT UPPER RIGHT CORNER OF PAGE 78. **9.** INSERT COPPER WIRE AS SHOWN. **10.** FINISH WITH SHOE POLISH AND ASSEMBLE AS SHOWN ABOVE.

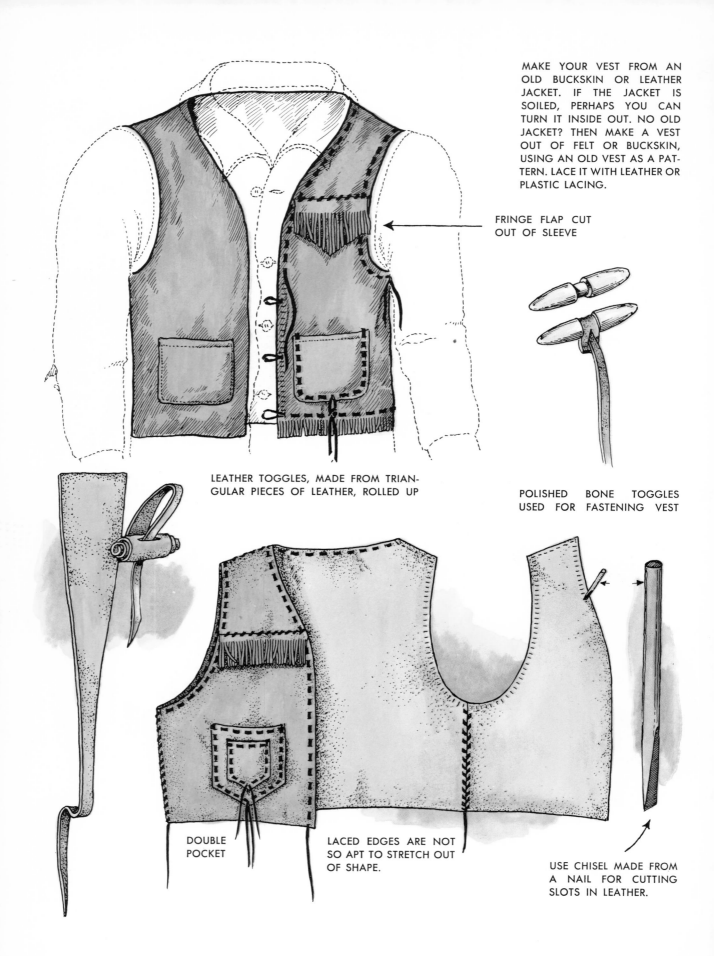

MAKE YOUR VEST FROM AN OLD BUCKSKIN OR LEATHER JACKET. IF THE JACKET IS SOILED, PERHAPS YOU CAN TURN IT INSIDE OUT. NO OLD JACKET? THEN MAKE A VEST OUT OF FELT OR BUCKSKIN, USING AN OLD VEST AS A PATTERN. LACE IT WITH LEATHER OR PLASTIC LACING.

FRINGE FLAP CUT OUT OF SLEEVE

LEATHER TOGGLES, MADE FROM TRIANGULAR PIECES OF LEATHER, ROLLED UP

POLISHED BONE TOGGLES USED FOR FASTENING VEST

DOUBLE POCKET

LACED EDGES ARE NOT SO APT TO STRETCH OUT OF SHAPE.

USE CHISEL MADE FROM A NAIL FOR CUTTING SLOTS IN LEATHER.

80

Emblem and Award Vest

Each year you acquire several awards and emblems from school, sports, and scouting activities. Then there is the problem of what to do with them. Some folks stash them away in a drawer, where they are forgotten. Others hang these trophies in their rooms where only a few friends can see them.

This vest was especially designed to display your awards and to keep them from getting lost. There is often quite a lot of activity at rallies and encampments in trading these emblems, and this vest makes a dandy showcase for what you have to trade.

Make your vest from an old buckskin or leather jacket, as shown on these two pages.

USE DOUBLE- OR SINGLE-THONG LACING FOR SIDE SEAMS AND SHOULDER SEAMS.

LACING

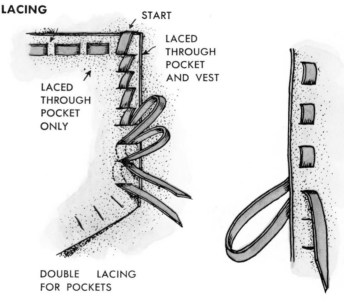

START

LACED THROUGH POCKET AND VEST

LACED THROUGH POCKET ONLY

DOUBLE LACING FOR POCKETS

USE SINGLE LACING ALONG EDGES OR FOR FASTENING POCKETS.

OVERCAST LACING

ENDS OF LEATHER LACING CAN BE FASTENED WITH CEMENT.

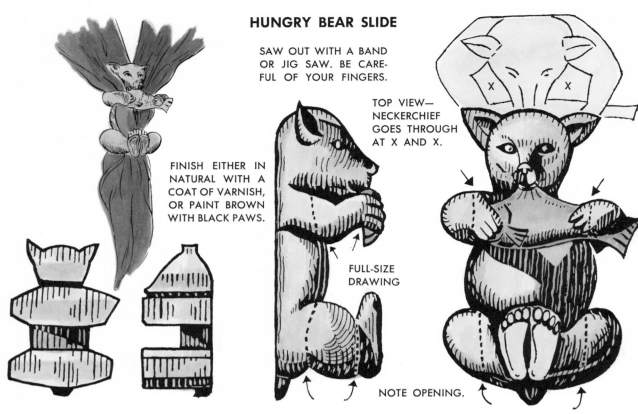

HUNGRY BEAR SLIDE

SAW OUT WITH A BAND OR JIG SAW. BE CAREFUL OF YOUR FINGERS.

FINISH EITHER IN NATURAL WITH A COAT OF VARNISH, OR PAINT BROWN WITH BLACK PAWS.

TOP VIEW—NECKERCHIEF GOES THROUGH AT X AND X.

FULL-SIZE DRAWING

NOTE OPENING.

Neckerchief Slides

The two easiest woods to whittle for neckerchief slides are white pine and basswood. The wood costs practically nothing, and the piece you need is so small you can carry it around in your pocket.

The knife that you use should be razor sharp. Watch your step and don't cut yourself. See page 5 for the correct handling of a pocketknife. A crooked knife is also very handy for carving neckerchief slides.

OLD WALRUS SLIDE

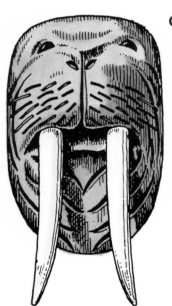

MAKE TUSKS OUT OF PLASTIC KNITTING NEEDLES. USE NYLON BRISTLES OF TOOTHBRUSH FOR WHISKERS.

GOUGE OUT BACK AND GLUE ON THE CROSS PIECE.

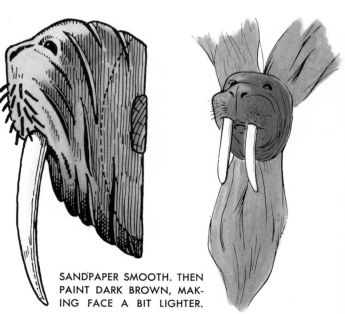

SANDPAPER SMOOTH. THEN PAINT DARK BROWN, MAKING FACE A BIT LIGHTER.

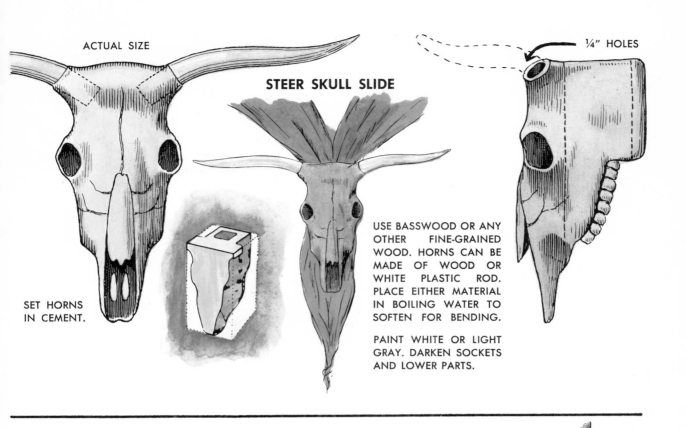

ACTUAL SIZE

STEER SKULL SLIDE

¼" HOLES

SET HORNS IN CEMENT.

USE BASSWOOD OR ANY OTHER FINE-GRAINED WOOD. HORNS CAN BE MADE OF WOOD OR WHITE PLASTIC ROD. PLACE EITHER MATERIAL IN BOILING WATER TO SOFTEN FOR BENDING.

PAINT WHITE OR LIGHT GRAY. DARKEN SOCKETS AND LOWER PARTS.

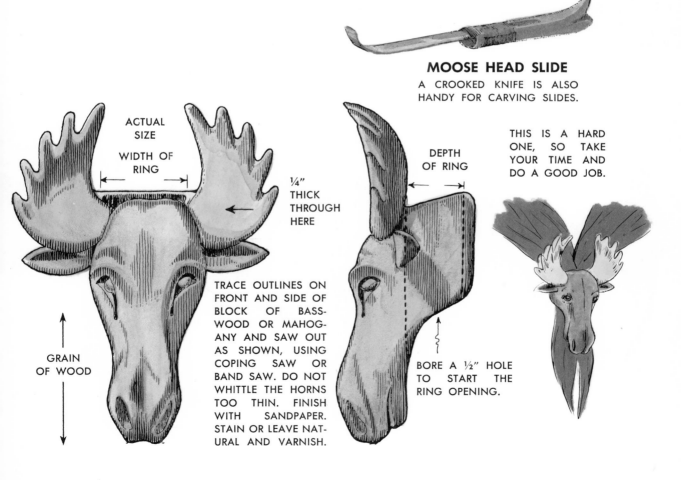

MOOSE HEAD SLIDE

A CROOKED KNIFE IS ALSO HANDY FOR CARVING SLIDES.

ACTUAL SIZE

WIDTH OF RING

¼" THICK THROUGH HERE

DEPTH OF RING

THIS IS A HARD ONE, SO TAKE YOUR TIME AND DO A GOOD JOB.

GRAIN OF WOOD

TRACE OUTLINES ON FRONT AND SIDE OF BLOCK OF BASS-WOOD OR MAHOG-ANY AND SAW OUT AS SHOWN, USING COPING SAW OR BAND SAW. DO NOT WHITTLE THE HORNS TOO THIN. FINISH WITH SANDPAPER. STAIN OR LEAVE NAT-URAL AND VARNISH.

BORE A ½" HOLE TO START THE RING OPENING.

Neckerchief Slides (*continued*)

HAND AX SLIDE

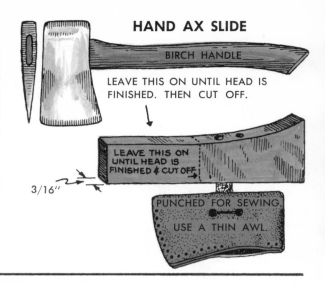

SHEATH OF THIN CALFSKIN SEWED WITH A SADDLE STITCH. LOOP OF 5/16" STRIP OF SAME CEMENTED TO SHEATH BACK THROUGH SLOTS.

THE AX-HEAD IS MADE OF ALUMINUM. IT CAN ALSO BE MADE OF BIRCH OR MAPLE AND PAINTED WITH ALUMINUM PAINT. DRILL TWO 1/16" HOLES TO START THE EYE. FILE OR WHITTLE OUT THE REST OF IT. CUT SLOTS BEFORE SEWING.

BIRCH HANDLE

LEAVE THIS ON UNTIL HEAD IS FINISHED. THEN CUT OFF.

LEAVE THIS ON UNTIL HEAD IS FINISHED & CUT OFF

3/16"

PUNCHED FOR SEWING. USE A THIN AWL.

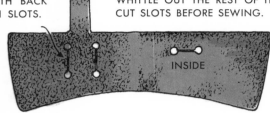

INSIDE

FULL SIZE OF AX AND SHEATH

BEADED THUNDERBIRD ROSETTE

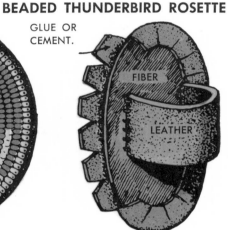

GLUE OR CEMENT.

FIBER

LEATHER

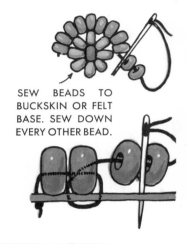

SEW BEADS TO BUCKSKIN OR FELT BASE. SEW DOWN EVERY OTHER BEAD.

RAINBOW TROUT SLIDE

WHITTLE THE LOOP FIRST. THAT'S THE TOUGHEST PART OF THIS SLIDE.

PRESS IN THE EYE WITH A LARGE NAIL SET.

ROUGH OUT A BLANK LIKE THIS TO START WITH.

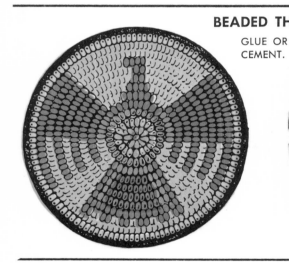

GET THE CORRECT COLORING FROM A GOOD BOOK AT THE LIBRARY.

FRONT VIEW

TOP VIEW

BACK

BOTTOM

DESIGNED BY J. S. KAY, CLEVELAND, O.

PAUL BUNYAN SLIDE

SINCE PAUL BUNYAN WAS SUCH A RUGGED FELLOW, LET THE KNIFE CUTS STAND. CUT THE SILHOUETTE OF THE SIDE VIEW FIRST. PAINT THE CAP, FACE, AND WHISKERS AS SHOWN HERE. CEMENT BLACK BEADS IN PLACE FOR THE EYES.

BACK VIEW SHOWING CROSS PIECE GLUED IN PLACE.

THE BEST WOOD TO USE FOR THIS SLIDE IS BAMBOO. SET CROSS PIECES INTO MORTISES. USE STRONG WHITE THREAD FOR THE WEBBING AND A BLUNT NEEDLE TO SAVE TIME. DRILL HOLES IN FRAME AFTER THE TAIL IS TIED. PAINT THE ENTIRE SLIDE WITH CLEAR LACQUER.

SNOWSHOE SLIDE

MAKE THE LOOP OF LEATHER AND SEW IT TO THE FRAME AT **A** AND **B**, AS SHOWN.

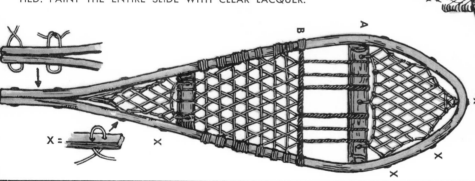

SET CROSS PIECES INTO THE FRAME.

INDIAN TEPEE SLIDE

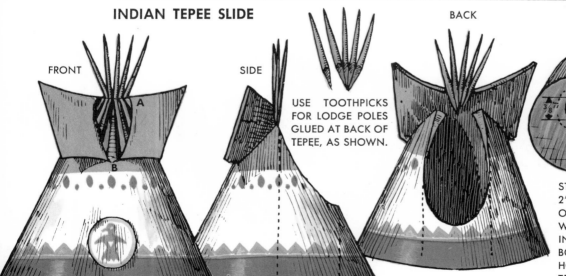

FRONT

SIDE

USE TOOTHPICKS FOR LODGE POLES GLUED AT BACK OF TEPEE, AS SHOWN.

BACK

START WITH A 2" CYLINDER OF SOFT WOOD, 2¼" IN DIAMETER. BORE A ⅜" HOLE. AFTER TEPEE IS ROUGHED OUT, ENLARGE HOLE TO ¾".

POLES AT SMOKE OPENING **A** TO **B** CAN BE WHITTLED OR PAINTED.

DON'T CUT SMOKE FLAPS TOO THIN. NOTICE THE POLES.

THIS VIEW SHOWS NECKERCHIEF OPENING AND POSITION OF POLES.

DEER OR ELK HORN BUTTONS
FOR BUCKSKIN OR FANCY SHIRTS AND COATS

FROM #4 PRONG

ROUGH EDGES

YOU CAN MAKE SMOOTH BUT-
TONS FROM THE SMOOTH
PRONGS. USE A HACK SAW.

#5

SAW OFF SLABS FROM WIDE SEC-
TIONS OR FROM LARGE PRONGS WITH
A HACK SAW OR ON A BAND SAW.

#6

SLABS UP TO 2" WIDE CAN BE SAWED FROM ELK HORN. BUTTONS CAN BE
FINISHED NATURAL; THEY CAN BE SCRAPED, FILED, AND FINISHED TO LOOK
LIKE IVORY; OR THEY CAN BE BURNED TO A RICH BROWN COLOR.

**1. USE BLOW
TORCH TO BURN
HORN TO A
DEEP BROWN.**

**2. GO OVER BURNT SURFACE WITH BOB
STICK TO REMOVE SURPLUS BURNT HORN.**

**3. SAW OFF
SECTIONS.**

**4. FILE
OFF ENDS.**

**5. FILE GROOVE AND
ROUND EDGES.**

FINISH ON BUFFING WHEEL OR
BOB STICK. RUB WITH BOILED
LINSEED OIL.

6. DRILL HOLES

TRY JIGGLE ENGRAVING ON
BONE AND DEER HORN.

BONE NECKERCHIEF SLIDES

DESIGNS ARE
SCRATCHED ON
WITH SHARP AWL
AND THEN INKED.

MADE FROM
HAM OR LEG
OF LAMB BONE

**TACK
ABRASIVE
BELOW.**

BOB STICK

FOR SMOOTHING HORN OR
BONE PRIOR TO POLISHING,
MAKE A BOB STICK. USE
FINE EMERY OR ANY OTHER
ABRASIVE CLOTH OVER A
PIECE OF ⅛" SPONGE RUB-
BER OR HEAVY INNER TUBE.
THIS ALSO MAKES A GOOD
KNIFE SHARPENER.

CRATE
LUMBER

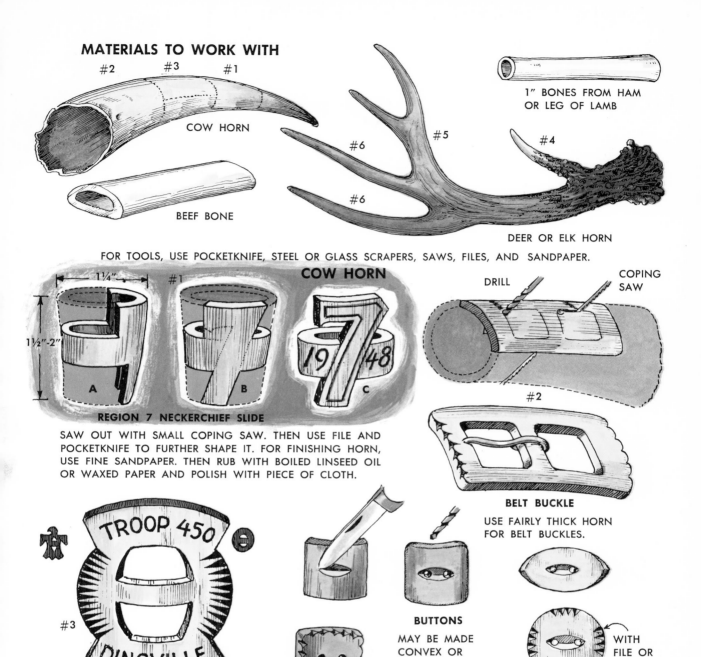

MATERIALS TO WORK WITH

#2 #3 #1

COW HORN

BEEF BONE

#6 #5 #6

1" BONES FROM HAM OR LEG OF LAMB

#4

DEER OR ELK HORN

FOR TOOLS, USE POCKETKNIFE, STEEL OR GLASS SCRAPERS, SAWS, FILES, AND SANDPAPER.

COW HORN

1¼"

#1

1½"-2"

19 7 48

A B C

REGION 7 NECKERCHIEF SLIDE

SAW OUT WITH SMALL COPING SAW. THEN USE FILE AND POCKETKNIFE TO FURTHER SHAPE IT. FOR FINISHING HORN, USE FINE SANDPAPER. THEN RUB WITH BOILED LINSEED OIL OR WAXED PAPER AND POLISH WITH PIECE OF CLOTH.

DRILL COPING SAW

#2

BELT BUCKLE

USE FAIRLY THICK HORN FOR BELT BUCKLES.

TROOP 450 DINGVILLE

#3

MANY OTHER SHAPES CAN BE USED FOR NECKERCHIEF SLIDES.

BUTTONS

MAY BE MADE CONVEX OR CONCAVE.

WITH FILE OR KNIFE

HORN AND BONE CAN ALSO BE POLISHED ON A CLEAN CLOTH BUFFING WHEEL CHARGED WITH BUFFING COMPOUND.

Bone and Horn Ornaments

Bones for craft projects can be cleaned in several ways. Cooked bones can be bleached by letting them lie in warm water for several days. Raw bones must be scraped and have all of the marrow removed. If you place them on an ant hill, the ants will do this for you quickly.

Designs should be engraved on the bones before polishing, as the texture of the rough bone keeps your engraving tool from slipping. About the only tools you will need are a hack saw, coping saw, pocketknife, file, drill, awl, and sandpaper.

THIS SHELL CAME FROM THE
WEST COAST OF FLORIDA.

PLANTER FOR MOTHER

IF YOU'RE LUCKY, YOU WON'T HAVE TO
DO MUCH WORK TO MAKE AN ATTRAC-
TIVE PLANTER. SOMETIMES THE DRIFT-
WOOD CAN STAND A CLEANING WITH
A STEEL BRUSH TO REMOVE DUST AND
ROTTED SPOTS. CUT OUT A DEPRESSION
TO FIT THE SHELL WITH A CROOKED
KNIFE AND SET THE SHELL IN A GOOD
COAT OF CEMENT. THEN LET IT DRY FOR
A COUPLE OF DAYS.

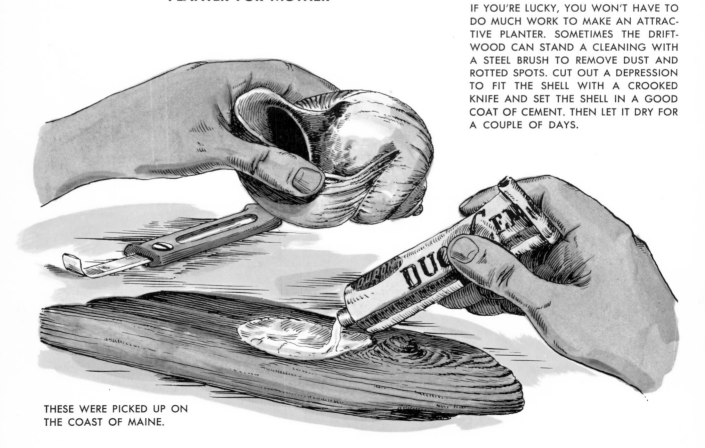

THESE WERE PICKED UP ON
THE COAST OF MAINE.

Shells and Driftwood

Few people can walk along the beach and pass up an interesting shell or piece of driftwood. Usually such finds are taken home, placed on a shelf, and forgotten. Whenever I find an unusual shell, however, I look around the same area for a nice piece of driftwood, or an old piece of gnarled wood. Then when I get home, I combine the two into planters or ash trays.

Before mounting your shell, test it very carefully with water to be sure it doesn't leak. Otherwise it won't hold ashes or dirt very well. For the planter, mix a little black dirt with peat moss and plant food. Place a sprig of ivy, cactus, or any other small green plant in the shell and water it when needed. In a few weeks you will have a nice gift for someone.

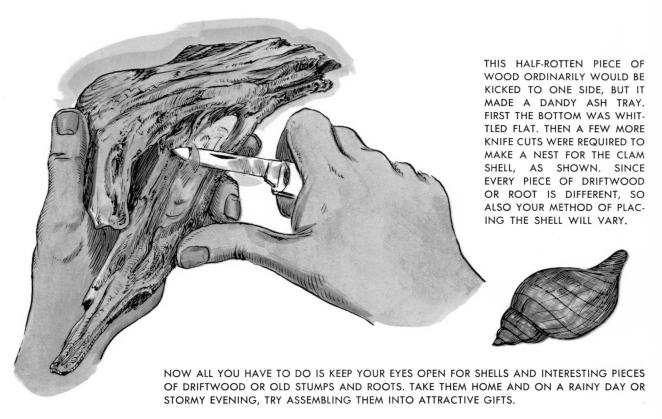

THIS HALF-ROTTEN PIECE OF WOOD ORDINARILY WOULD BE KICKED TO ONE SIDE, BUT IT MADE A DANDY ASH TRAY. FIRST THE BOTTOM WAS WHITTLED FLAT. THEN A FEW MORE KNIFE CUTS WERE REQUIRED TO MAKE A NEST FOR THE CLAM SHELL, AS SHOWN. SINCE EVERY PIECE OF DRIFTWOOD OR ROOT IS DIFFERENT, SO ALSO YOUR METHOD OF PLACING THE SHELL WILL VARY.

NOW ALL YOU HAVE TO DO IS KEEP YOUR EYES OPEN FOR SHELLS AND INTERESTING PIECES OF DRIFTWOOD OR OLD STUMPS AND ROOTS. TAKE THEM HOME AND ON A RAINY DAY OR STORMY EVENING, TRY ASSEMBLING THEM INTO ATTRACTIVE GIFTS.

ASH TRAY FOR DAD

THIS IS AN ODD COMBINATION. THE WOOD CAME FROM THE JAMBOREE AT IRVINE RANCH AND THE CLAM SHELL CAME FROM NORTHERN WISCONSIN.

Wooden Bowls and Noggins

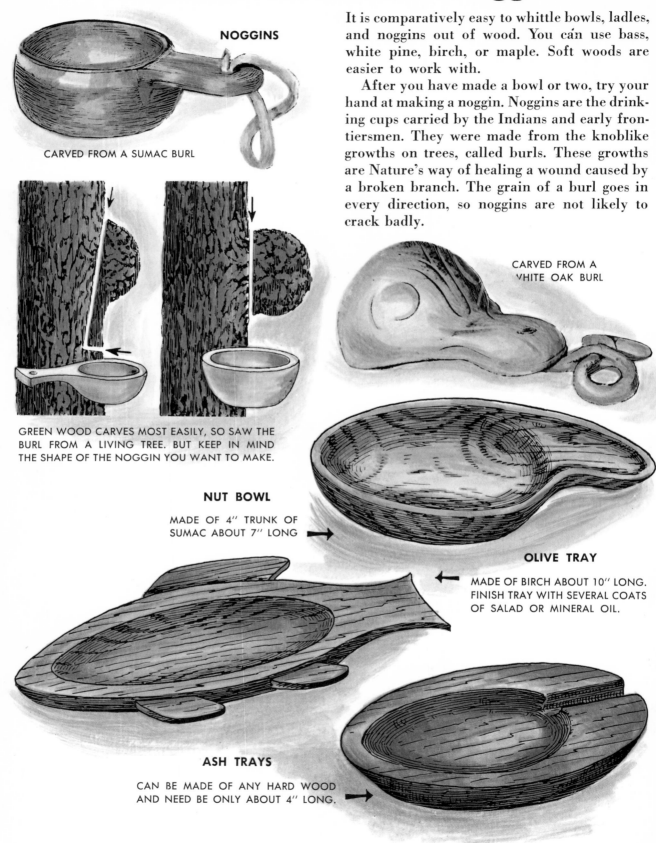

It is comparatively easy to whittle bowls, ladles, and noggins out of wood. You cán use bass, white pine, birch, or maple. Soft woods are easier to work with.

After you have made a bowl or two, try your hand at making a noggin. Noggins are the drinking cups carried by the Indians and early frontiersmen. They were made from the knoblike growths on trees, called burls. These growths are Nature's way of healing a wound caused by a broken branch. The grain of a burl goes in every direction, so noggins are not likely to crack badly.

NOGGINS

CARVED FROM A SUMAC BURL

GREEN WOOD CARVES MOST EASILY, SO SAW THE BURL FROM A LIVING TREE. BUT KEEP IN MIND THE SHAPE OF THE NOGGIN YOU WANT TO MAKE.

CARVED FROM A WHITE OAK BURL

NUT BOWL

MADE OF 4" TRUNK OF SUMAC ABOUT 7" LONG ➤

OLIVE TRAY

◄ MADE OF BIRCH ABOUT 10" LONG. FINISH TRAY WITH SEVERAL COATS OF SALAD OR MINERAL OIL.

ASH TRAYS

CAN BE MADE OF ANY HARD WOOD AND NEED BE ONLY ABOUT 4" LONG. ➤

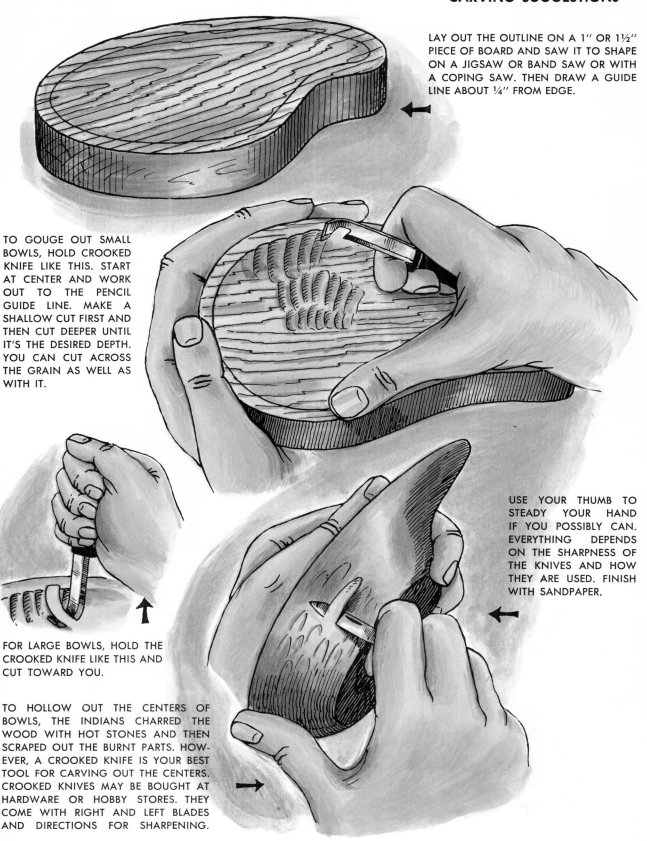

CARVING SUGGESTIONS

LAY OUT THE OUTLINE ON A 1" OR 1½" PIECE OF BOARD AND SAW IT TO SHAPE ON A JIGSAW OR BAND SAW OR WITH A COPING SAW. THEN DRAW A GUIDE LINE ABOUT ¼" FROM EDGE.

TO GOUGE OUT SMALL BOWLS, HOLD CROOKED KNIFE LIKE THIS. START AT CENTER AND WORK OUT TO THE PENCIL GUIDE LINE. MAKE A SHALLOW CUT FIRST AND THEN CUT DEEPER UNTIL IT'S THE DESIRED DEPTH. YOU CAN CUT ACROSS THE GRAIN AS WELL AS WITH IT.

USE YOUR THUMB TO STEADY YOUR HAND IF YOU POSSIBLY CAN. EVERYTHING DEPENDS ON THE SHARPNESS OF THE KNIVES AND HOW THEY ARE USED. FINISH WITH SANDPAPER.

FOR LARGE BOWLS, HOLD THE CROOKED KNIFE LIKE THIS AND CUT TOWARD YOU.

TO HOLLOW OUT THE CENTERS OF BOWLS, THE INDIANS CHARRED THE WOOD WITH HOT STONES AND THEN SCRAPED OUT THE BURNT PARTS. HOWEVER, A CROOKED KNIFE IS YOUR BEST TOOL FOR CARVING OUT THE CENTERS. CROOKED KNIVES MAY BE BOUGHT AT HARDWARE OR HOBBY STORES. THEY COME WITH RIGHT AND LEFT BLADES AND DIRECTIONS FOR SHARPENING.

FROM NUT SHELLS

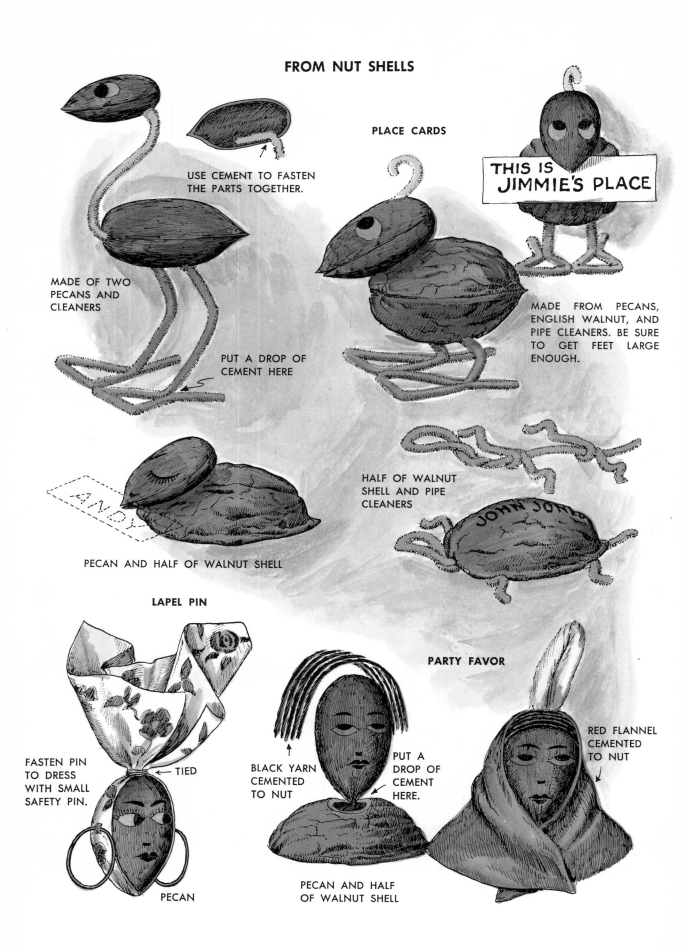

USE CEMENT TO FASTEN THE PARTS TOGETHER.

PLACE CARDS

THIS IS JIMMIE'S PLACE

MADE OF TWO PECANS AND CLEANERS

PUT A DROP OF CEMENT HERE

MADE FROM PECANS, ENGLISH WALNUT, AND PIPE CLEANERS. BE SURE TO GET FEET LARGE ENOUGH.

HALF OF WALNUT SHELL AND PIPE CLEANERS

ANDY

JOHN JONES

PECAN AND HALF OF WALNUT SHELL

LAPEL PIN

FASTEN PIN TO DRESS WITH SMALL SAFETY PIN.

TIED

PECAN

PARTY FAVOR

BLACK YARN CEMENTED TO NUT

PUT A DROP OF CEMENT HERE.

RED FLANNEL CEMENTED TO NUT

PECAN AND HALF OF WALNUT SHELL

Nut Craft

A lot of amusing trinkets can be made out of a bowl of mixed nuts with some glue, pipe cleaners, and a feather or two. Peach and plum pits and coconut shells can also be used for carving small objects.

Nut craft is a good hobby for cub scouts and brownies, as the raw materials are easily obtained and the projects are simple to do.

FROM PEACH AND PLUM PITS

CARVED MONKEY

TO WHITTLE THE MONKEY, CUT THE PEACH PIT DOWN RATHER SMOOTH AND THEN DRAW OUTLINE.

PLUM PIT BASKET

SIDE VIEW

FRONT VIEW

PEACH PIT BASKET

YOU'LL NEED A GOOD, SHARP KNIFE FOR THESE.

FROM COCONUT SHELLS

NOGGIN

USE FILE AND SANDPAPER FOR SMOOTHING SURFACE. POLISH WITH SALAD OIL AND CLOTH.

NECKERCHIEF SLIDES

MADE FROM PIECES OF A COCONUT SHELL AND DECORATED WITH "V" CUTS. THE LEATHER LOOP IS CEMENTED TO BACK.

FRONT VIEW

SIDE VIEW

ADAPTER—
SOLDER TO
TOP OF CAN

TOBACCO CAN

WOODEN
PLUGS FOR
JUGS AND
BOTTLES

MOLASSES JUG

**VINEGAR
JUG**

SOLDER
ADAPTER
TO THE
COVER.

GLASS BOTTLES

LET ORANGE PAINT RUN
DOWN INSIDE. WHEN DRY,
SWISH BLACK PAINT ALL
OVER INSIDE OF BOTTLE.

TIN CANS

OPEN ENDS
AT BOTTOM

WOOD
BASES

CANS ARE HELD TO BASE WITH
⅛" PIPE AND NUTS.

FINISH WITH ENAMEL
PAINTS AND DECALS.

Antique Lamps

Interesting lamps can be made from odd-shaped bottles, tin cans, jugs, pieces of wood, a very little work, and a lot of imagination. This is a good money-making project. Make up a half dozen lamps and you will be surprised at how fast you can sell them if you do a good job. Keep your eyes open when you go through your attic or barn. Whenever you see something which has been discarded, try to visualize it made up into a lamp.

POWDER HORN LAMPS

WOODEN PLUG

1" NIPPLE OF ³⁄₈" PIPE (CALLED ⅛")

BIRCH OR CHERRY LOG

WOOD BASE

METHOD OF FASTENING HORN TO BASE. DRILL SMALL LEAD HOLES.

BASE

HOLE FOR CORD

LEAD HOLE FOR LARGE SCREW

CORD OUTLET

POWDER HORN ATTACHMENT

(LOOKING UP FROM BENEATH)

OLD OIL LAMP

ANOTHER TYPE OF ADAPTER

OLD OIL LAMPS CAN BE WIRED WITH THE AID OF ADAPTERS THAT SCREW INTO THE ORIGINAL SOCKETS. ADAPTERS COME IN VARIOUS SIZES.

LIGHT-WEIGHT LAMPS AND SOME BOTTLE LAMPS REQUIRE HEAVY BASES OR A SAND OR PLASTER-OF-PARIS BALLAST TO MAKE THEM STAND FIRM. USE OLD SHADES FOR WIRE FRAME AND FOR PATTERN OF NEW PAPER FRAME.

Tepee Tom-tom Lamp

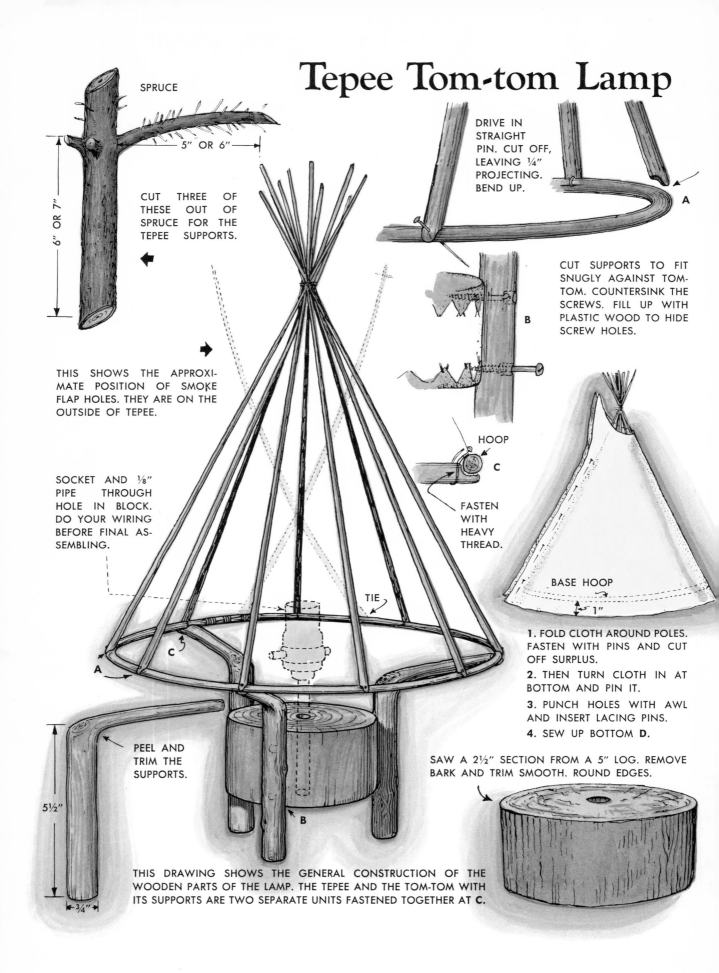

SPRUCE

← 5" OR 6" →

6" OR 7"

CUT THREE OF THESE OUT OF SPRUCE FOR THE TEPEE SUPPORTS.

DRIVE IN STRAIGHT PIN. CUT OFF, LEAVING ¼" PROJECTING. BEND UP.

A

CUT SUPPORTS TO FIT SNUGLY AGAINST TOM-TOM. COUNTERSINK THE SCREWS. FILL UP WITH PLASTIC WOOD TO HIDE SCREW HOLES.

B

THIS SHOWS THE APPROXIMATE POSITION OF SMOKE FLAP HOLES. THEY ARE ON THE OUTSIDE OF TEPEE.

HOOP

C

FASTEN WITH HEAVY THREAD.

SOCKET AND ⅛" PIPE THROUGH HOLE IN BLOCK. DO YOUR WIRING BEFORE FINAL ASSEMBLING.

TIE

C

A

BASE HOOP

1"

1. FOLD CLOTH AROUND POLES. FASTEN WITH PINS AND CUT OFF SURPLUS.

2. THEN TURN CLOTH IN AT BOTTOM AND PIN IT.

3. PUNCH HOLES WITH AWL AND INSERT LACING PINS.

4. SEW UP BOTTOM **D**.

PEEL AND TRIM THE SUPPORTS.

5½"

¾"

B

SAW A 2½" SECTION FROM A 5" LOG. REMOVE BARK AND TRIM SMOOTH. ROUND EDGES.

THIS DRAWING SHOWS THE GENERAL CONSTRUCTION OF THE WOODEN PARTS OF THE LAMP. THE TEPEE AND THE TOM-TOM WITH ITS SUPPORTS ARE TWO SEPARATE UNITS FASTENED TOGETHER AT C.

CUT HOLES THROUGH COVER WHEN DRY.

TOM-TOM BASE

LACE WET BUCKSKIN OR THIN WET RAW-HIDE OVER BLOCK. WHEN DRY, DECORATE WITH WATER COLORS OR DULL OIL PAINTS.

DOOR

CUT OUT DOOR AFTER LACING AND SEWING. MAKE DOOR FLAP BY SEWING A PIECE OF MUSLIN OVER A THIN WILLOW HOOP. FASTEN DOOR WITH "PIN" AT TOP AND SEW IT AT THE BOTTOM.

SELECT TWELVE WILLOW SHOOTS 18" LONG AND ¼" AT THE BUTTS. PEEL AND STRAIGHTEN THEM. WRAP WITH CORD AND HANG UP TO DRY.

SELECT ONE STRAIGHT WILLOW SHOOT 3½' TO 4' LONG. PEEL, AND TRIM THE BUTT END HALFWAY UP TO EVEN THICKNESS. WHILE STILL GREEN, BEND IT AROUND A 12" CYLINDER AND TIE. LET IT DRY FOR A COUPLE OF DAYS.

WHEN DRY, MAKE SPLICE AS SHOWN, USING GLUE AND HEAVY THREAD.

4" SPLICE

THORNS MAKE GOOD LACING PINS.

KEEP TAUT.

D

SEWING CLOTH TO DOOR HOOP (INNER SIDE)

TEPEE SHADE

DOOR FLAP

FINISHED LAMP

Stamping Tools

The most highly prized possession of an Indian silversmith is his collection of hand-made stamps and punches, used to stamp the designs onto the metal after it is cut into shape. You will need to make yourself a set of these tools. 40- or 60-penny spikes work very well on soft aluminum. The other tools you will need are a small cold chisel, jewelry saw, mechanic's hammer, several small three-needle files, a mallet, and a bench vise.

SOME TYPICAL INDIAN DESIGNS

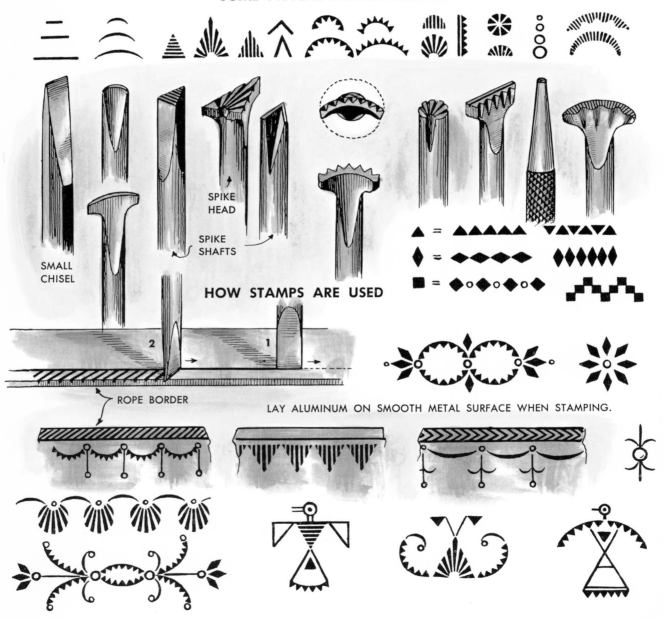

SMALL CHISEL

SPIKE HEAD

SPIKE SHAFTS

HOW STAMPS ARE USED

2   1

ROPE BORDER

LAY ALUMINUM ON SMOOTH METAL SURFACE WHEN STAMPING.

HOW TO MAKE STAMPS

USE A MEDIUM-WEIGHT, BALL-PEEN HAMMER FOR STAMPING. PLACE THE WORK ON A SMOOTH IRON SURFACE, SUCH AS AN ANVIL OR AN OLD-FASHIONED FLAT IRON.

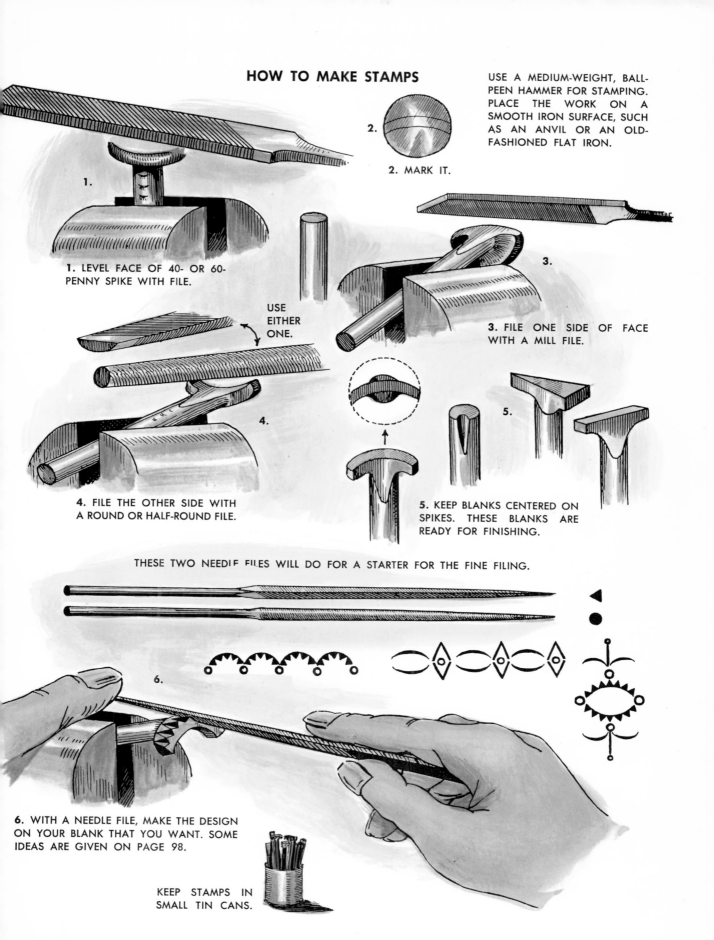

2. MARK IT.

1. LEVEL FACE OF 40- OR 60-PENNY SPIKE WITH FILE.

USE EITHER ONE.

3. FILE ONE SIDE OF FACE WITH A MILL FILE.

4. FILE THE OTHER SIDE WITH A ROUND OR HALF-ROUND FILE.

5. KEEP BLANKS CENTERED ON SPIKES. THESE BLANKS ARE READY FOR FINISHING.

THESE TWO NEEDLE FILES WILL DO FOR A STARTER FOR THE FINE FILING.

6.

6. WITH A NEEDLE FILE, MAKE THE DESIGN ON YOUR BLANK THAT YOU WANT. SOME IDEAS ARE GIVEN ON PAGE 98.

KEEP STAMPS IN SMALL TIN CANS.

Belt Buckles

In our great Southwest the Navajo and Pueblo Indians are noted for their beautiful silver jewelry. Some of the pieces are very difficult to make and require years of experience. However, other flat pieces, such as belt buckles and bracelets, are quite easy for beginners to make if they have the proper tools.

Silver is rather expensive and hard to work with, so I have worked out several pieces that can be made in 14-gauge aluminum.

1. TRACE THIS DESIGN AND TRANSFER IT ONTO A PIECE OF 14-GAUGE ALUMINUM. CUT WHAT YOU CAN WITH A TIN SHEARS AND SAW THE REST WITH A JEWELER'S SAW, A COPING SAW, OR ON A JIG SAW. FILE EDGES SMOOTH.

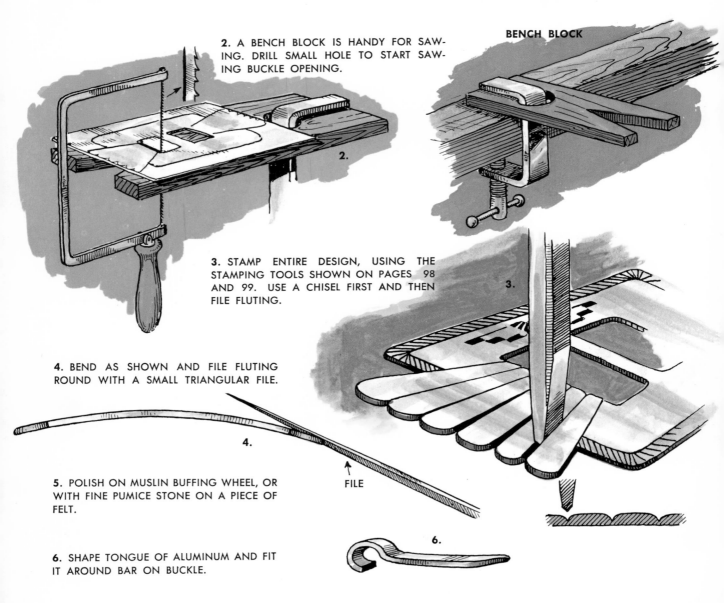

2. A BENCH BLOCK IS HANDY FOR SAWING. DRILL SMALL HOLE TO START SAWING BUCKLE OPENING.

BENCH BLOCK

3. STAMP ENTIRE DESIGN, USING THE STAMPING TOOLS SHOWN ON PAGES 98 AND 99. USE A CHISEL FIRST AND THEN FILE FLUTING.

4. BEND AS SHOWN AND FILE FLUTING ROUND WITH A SMALL TRIANGULAR FILE.

FILE

5. POLISH ON MUSLIN BUFFING WHEEL, OR WITH FINE PUMICE STONE ON A PIECE OF FELT.

6. SHAPE TONGUE OF ALUMINUM AND FIT IT AROUND BAR ON BUCKLE.

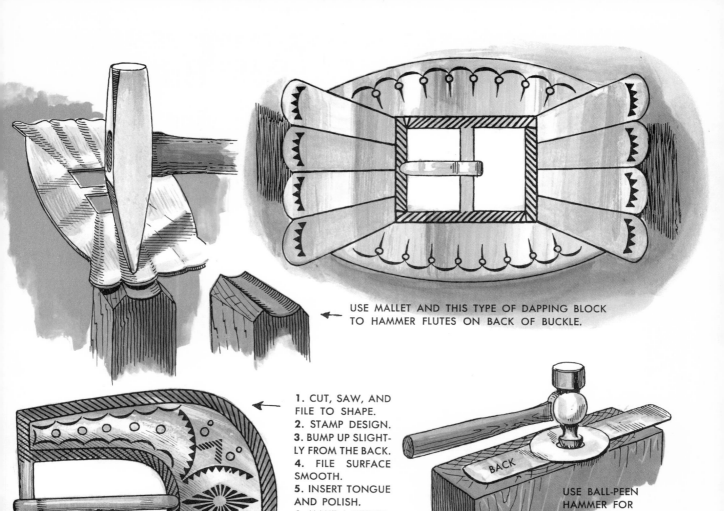

USE MALLET AND THIS TYPE OF DAPPING BLOCK TO HAMMER FLUTES ON BACK OF BUCKLE.

1. CUT, SAW, AND FILE TO SHAPE.
2. STAMP DESIGN.
3. BUMP UP SLIGHTLY FROM THE BACK.
4. FILE SURFACE SMOOTH.
5. INSERT TONGUE AND POLISH.
6. MAKE A KEEPER.

USE BALL-PEEN HAMMER FOR BUMPING UP.

BACK

KEEPER

USE DAPPING PUNCHES MADE OF BRASS OR IRON AND A DAPPING BLOCK TO SHAPE THE CIRCLES AND ELLIPSES SHOWN ON THIS BUCKLE.

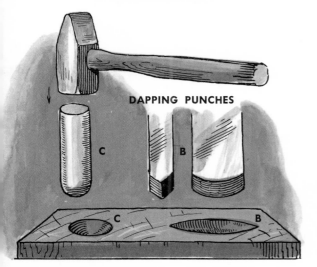

DAPPING PUNCHES

C   B

C   B

DAPPING BLOCK OF HARDWOOD

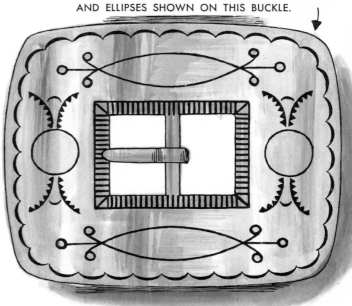

Aluminum Bracelets

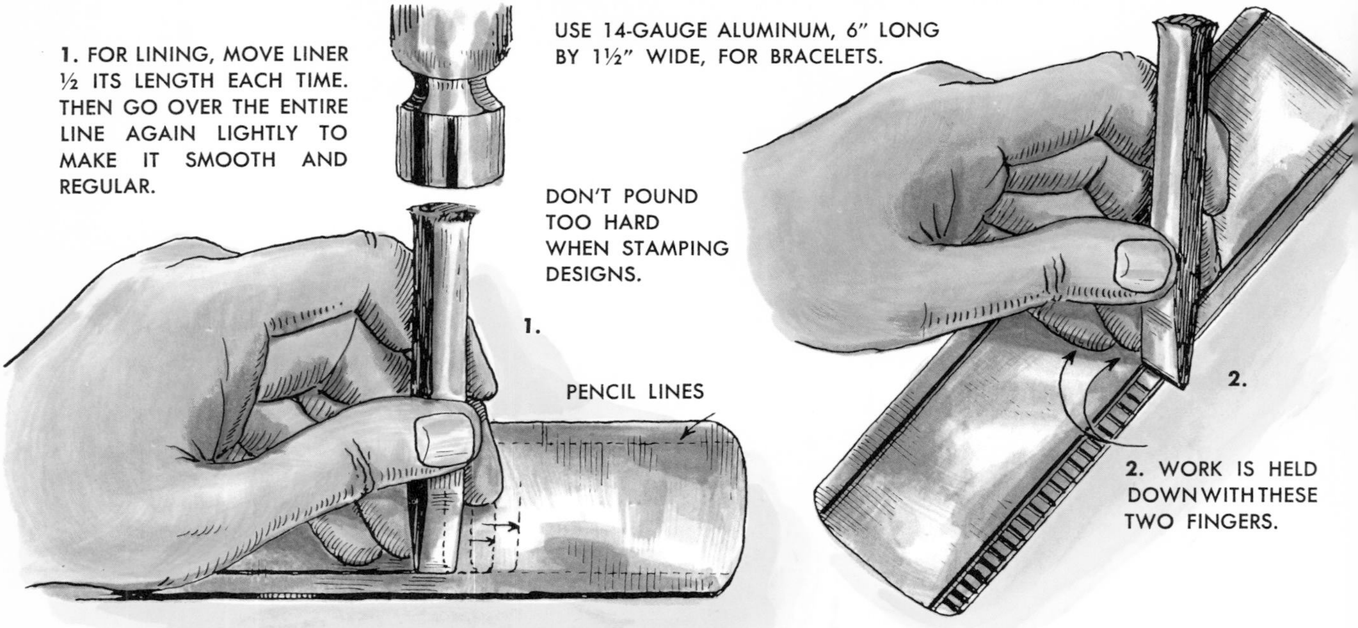

USE 14-GAUGE ALUMINUM, 6" LONG BY 1½" WIDE, FOR BRACELETS.

1. FOR LINING, MOVE LINER ½ ITS LENGTH EACH TIME. THEN GO OVER THE ENTIRE LINE AGAIN LIGHTLY TO MAKE IT SMOOTH AND REGULAR.

DON'T POUND TOO HARD WHEN STAMPING DESIGNS.

1.

PENCIL LINES

2.

2. WORK IS HELD DOWN WITH THESE TWO FINGERS.

BRACELET WITH BUILT-UP EDGES

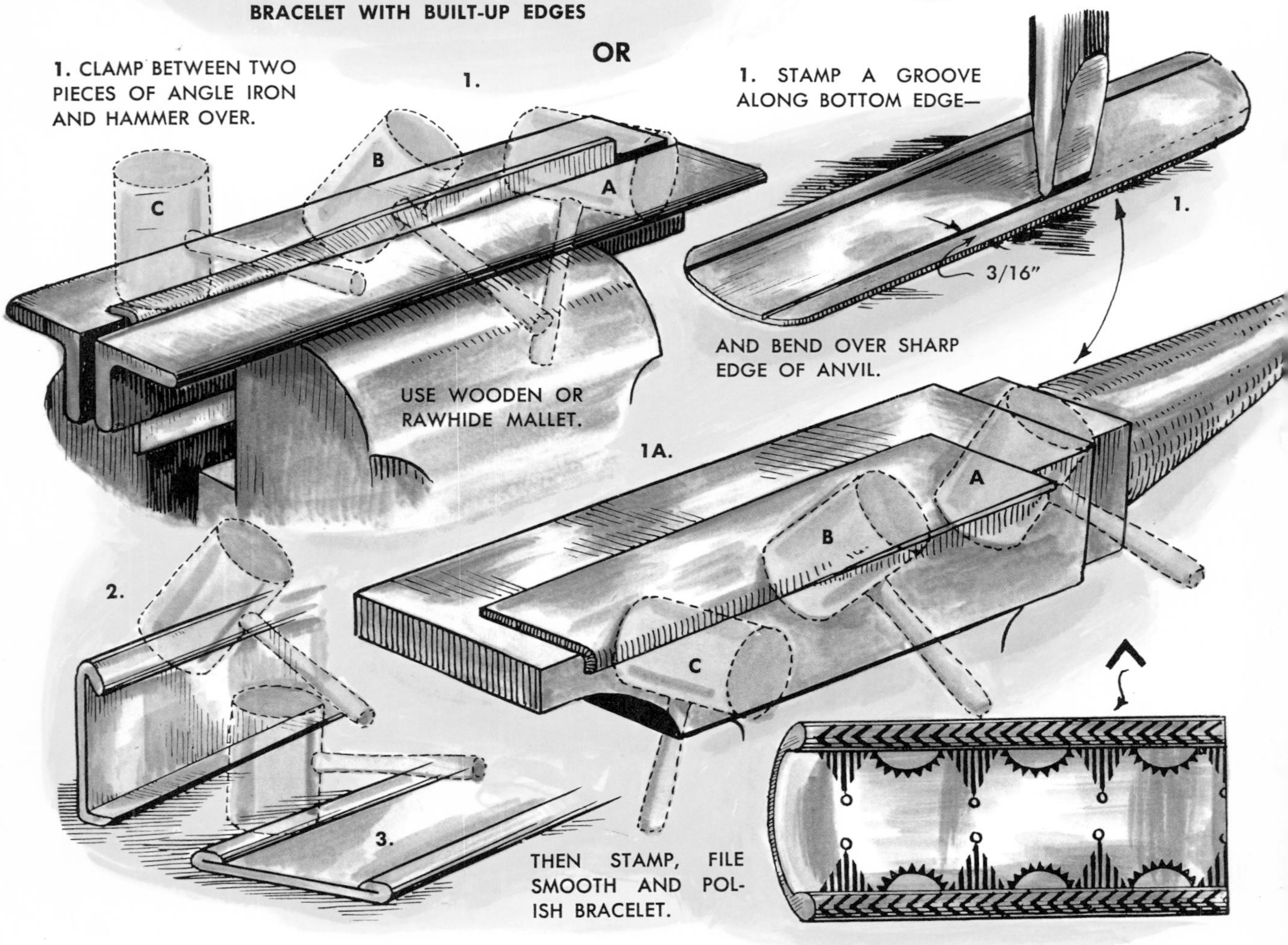

OR

1. CLAMP BETWEEN TWO PIECES OF ANGLE IRON AND HAMMER OVER.

1.

B

A

C

USE WOODEN OR RAWHIDE MALLET.

1. STAMP A GROOVE ALONG BOTTOM EDGE—

1.

3/16"

AND BEND OVER SHARP EDGE OF ANVIL.

1A.

A

B

C

2.

3.

THEN STAMP, FILE SMOOTH AND POLISH BRACELET.

102

THESE BRACELETS ARE A LITTLE MORE DIFFICULT TO MAKE, AND AT THE SAME TIME, THEY ARE MORE ATTRACTIVE. SIX INCHES IS THE STANDARD LENGTH OF BRACELETS.

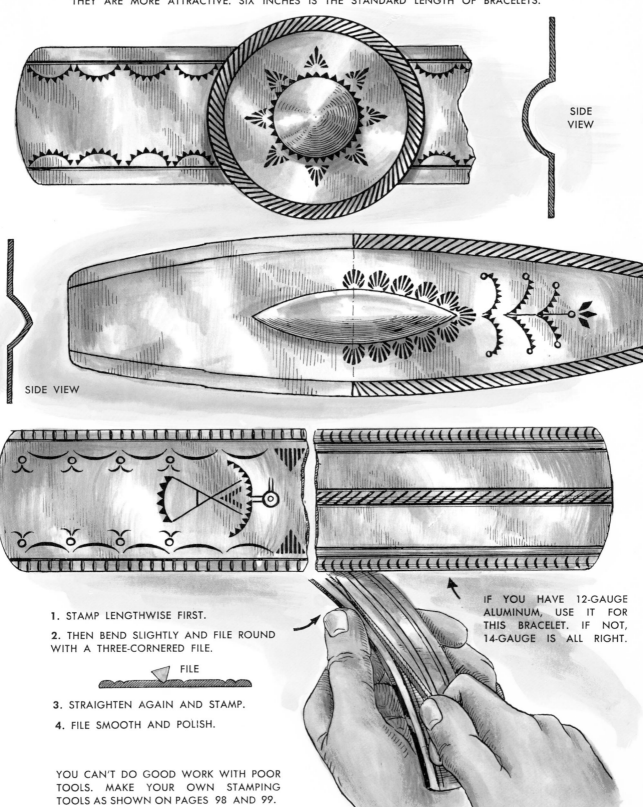

SIDE VIEW

SIDE VIEW

1. STAMP LENGTHWISE FIRST.

2. THEN BEND SLIGHTLY AND FILE ROUND WITH A THREE-CORNERED FILE.

FILE

3. STRAIGHTEN AGAIN AND STAMP.

4. FILE SMOOTH AND POLISH.

YOU CAN'T DO GOOD WORK WITH POOR TOOLS. MAKE YOUR OWN STAMPING TOOLS AS SHOWN ON PAGES 98 AND 99.

IF YOU HAVE 12-GAUGE ALUMINUM, USE IT FOR THIS BRACELET. IF NOT, 14-GAUGE IS ALL RIGHT.

INDEX